KAFFE FASSETT
passionate patchwork

KAFFE FASSETT
with Liza Prior Lucy

passionate patchwork

Over 20 original quilt designs

Photography by Debbie Patterson

The Taunton Press

First published 2001

1 3 5 7 9 10 8 6 4 2

Text and patchwork designs copyright © Kaffe Fassett 2001
Photography copyright © Debbie Patterson 2001
(except photographs listed in credits on page 158)

The Taunton Press
Inspiration for hands-on living™

First published in the United Kingdom in 2001
by Ebury Press, Random House
20 Vauxhall Bridge Road, London SW1V 2SA
www.randomhouse.co.uk

The Taunton Press, Inc.
63 South Main St.
PO Box 5506
Newtown, CT 06470-5506
www.taunton.com

Distributed by Publishers Group West

Editor Sally Harding
Art Director Polly Dawes
Photographer Debbie Patterson
Copy Editor Ali Glenny
Patchwork flat shot photography Jon Stewart
Patchwork instruction diagrams Ethan Danielson
Techniques illustrations Kate Simunek

ISBN 1-56158-438-X

Color separation by Colorlito, Milan
Printed and bound in Singapore by Tien Wah Press

contents

introduction

'What are you gong to tackle next?' is so often flung at me after I've just given a slide show and talk. The audience will just have witnessed me having a go at knitting, needlepoint, rag rugs, patchwork and mosaic. Since I perceive all these as the same – playing with patterns and colours – the image some must have of me being a dilettante doesn't enter my mind. However, the desire to concentrate on and delve deeper into each of these media

THIS PAGE AND NEXT PAGE A new ground of flower prints beautifully integrates the antique medallions (above) and pieces of Wedding Ring patchwork (right) on our *Medallion Circles* quilt. Yoyos add texture around the border.

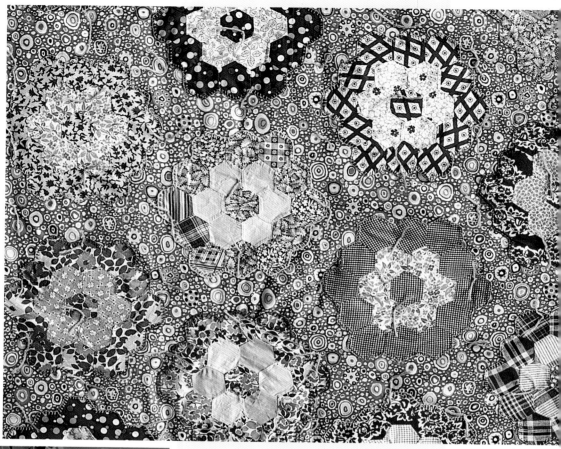

RIGHT AND BELOW The hand-sewn antique blocks on my *Granny's Flower Garden* quilt nestle deliciously into my *Roman Glass* print. Even though the fabrics in the medallions are very ordinary, they become mysteriously appealing in the larger composition of the quilt. (See page 149 for how to make quilts with antique blocks.) OPPOSITE PAGE The old-fashioned English borders of the garden at Parham House in West Sussex reflect this subtle balance.

does overpower me from time to time.

This book, developed with my trusty co-author Liza, was therefore highly satisfying to both of us. We would be able to expand on ideas that were sparked off by our first patchwork book. Initially, we spent days poring over books on exhibitions of old quilts, never tiring of their highly inspiring content. It won't have escaped patchwork aficionados that I borrow heavily from classic old geometry. My logic tells me 'why strive for complicated, difficult-to-sew arrangements when simple squares, diamonds and triangles are so endlessly fascinating as long as the colours are alive'.

Working with circles has proved slightly more complex. It brought

appliqué into my patchwork vocabulary for the first time (see pages 19 and 21). What a joy a circle is! And the stitchers of this world tell me that appliqué is not difficult to master.

Here I have to remind everyone that I don't sew. Liza Lucy works at my side cutting patches for me to arrange in the layout of each new quilt design. She then sews them together and arranges for the quilting. This makes a shared experience of the potentially arduous task of designing and also ensures that the seams meet with precision. We work as a team, from planning, to shopping for fabric, working out new fabric designs and colourways for my patchwork fabric collection, and making decisions about bindings and stitch colours on quilting.

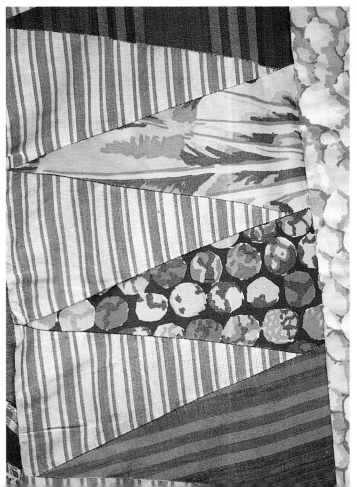

I arrive for designing and shopping at Liza's home in Pennsylvania from my London studio for a week or two at a time. We convert Liza's dining room into a workroom with four big design walls. Each wall is a large insulation board covered with camel-toned flannel. I arrange my patchwork on these boards, and can rearrange easily, as the small cotton patches stick to the flannel. You can see from my notes on each quilt how ideas for colour or layout come from many sources. When the quilt and border are just the way I like them, we take a

LEFT AND OPPOSITE PAGE The antique stars on *String Stars* are so strong that they survive my *Beads* print background. Our modern border of soft flags uses my *Blue and White Stripe* as a ground, and antique Wedding Ring blocks form the outer border. BELOW I bought this vintage quilt top and the stars for *String Stars* at the Houston International Quilt Festival.

photo and carefully pick up the patches for Liza to sew together when I've left. In this way we design about eight ideas at a go. Some later get dropped if they prove less than thrilling when completed.

One of the most exciting things I did for this book was to delve into the world

of incorporating antique patch blocks into quilts. Liza and I have dug through boxes and boxes of old unfinished patchwork at Houston's International Quilt Festival. Vendors come to this market from all over the world, but mostly from the midwest and south of the United States. They bring old patchwork tops or just bundles of blocks that were meticulously sewn together to become part of someone's bright idea for a quilt. Either the creator of these died, or just got distracted. All that work will have gone to waste if someone else doesn't take these blocks and build a quilt around them. I can't tell you how stimulating it is to do just that!

I used antique blocks in my *Medallion Circles*, *Granny's Flower Garden* and *String Stars* (see pages 7, 9 and 11). They were a joy to place on patterned ground and

ABOVE AND RIGHT Here's a great patchwork idea for a beginner knitter – squares of stripes in contrasting cotton yarns that are crocheted together. I chose a red-orange bias for my version, which creates a spark on this kelly-green caravan. OPPOSITE PAGE This antique quilt top was purchased from a collector in California. The Handkerchief Corner blocks are made up of such jaunty prints. I can look at this patchwork for hours and find new patterns each time.

build borders for. There is a zany almost primitive freedom in these old blocks that inspires me to try my own sewing one of these days.

Most exciting for me in this book – after the colour, which is always my deepest thrill – is getting into appliqué for the first time. What freedom to manage the circles and pot shapes that have always been close to my heart! You can see in my book *Glorious Colour* how obsessed I've been with ceramics in the V&A Museum in London and how I've used them in my needlepoint and knitting. For *Glorious Interiors* I even made a rag rug and ceramic tiles covered with pot shapes. If you are ever at a loss for ideas and share my love of colourful pots, do visit the top floor of the V&A, where all the ceramics of the world are represented in an outstanding collection.

As usual when I bring out a book, my mind races ahead to imagine what you, the reader and practitioner, will make of these colours and patch formats. With Liza and my assistant Brandon, I have given workshops all over the world based on the *Rosy* quilt from my first patchwork book. The sheer number of variations and individual approaches to a simple layout are always astounding. Visiting the world's quilt shops I'm forever curious to see how someone has done their own thing with my fabrics or layouts.

Now I'm itching to see how the appliqué bowls, for instance, are interpreted (see page 15). You will notice

that whenever possible I've worked out an alternative colour mood for my designs – in the case of the *Garden* quilts, four colourways. This is to encourage many more variations on each idea. So go on, surprise me! I know you will.

round and round

FOR MY FIRST BOOK, *Glorious Knitting*, I came up with a knitting design called *Persian Poppy* that hit a nerve with the public. It was simply staggered rows of striped circles with a contrasting centre in each of them. Everywhere I go in the world, I see scores of delightful versions of this little circular design. Circles recur at regular intervals in all the various media I work in. I have long wanted to play with curved shapes in patchwork but was shy of appliqué, feeling it would be too complicated. Now that Liza and I have finally attempted this delicious technique, I feel liberated, and the ideas for circular motifs are coming to me thick and fast.

RIGHT The simple primitive shape of the bowls and the happy circles of colour in the border make the *Dark Rice Bowls Hanging* a design that is at home in a modern house or a traditional one. (See page 72 for instructions.)

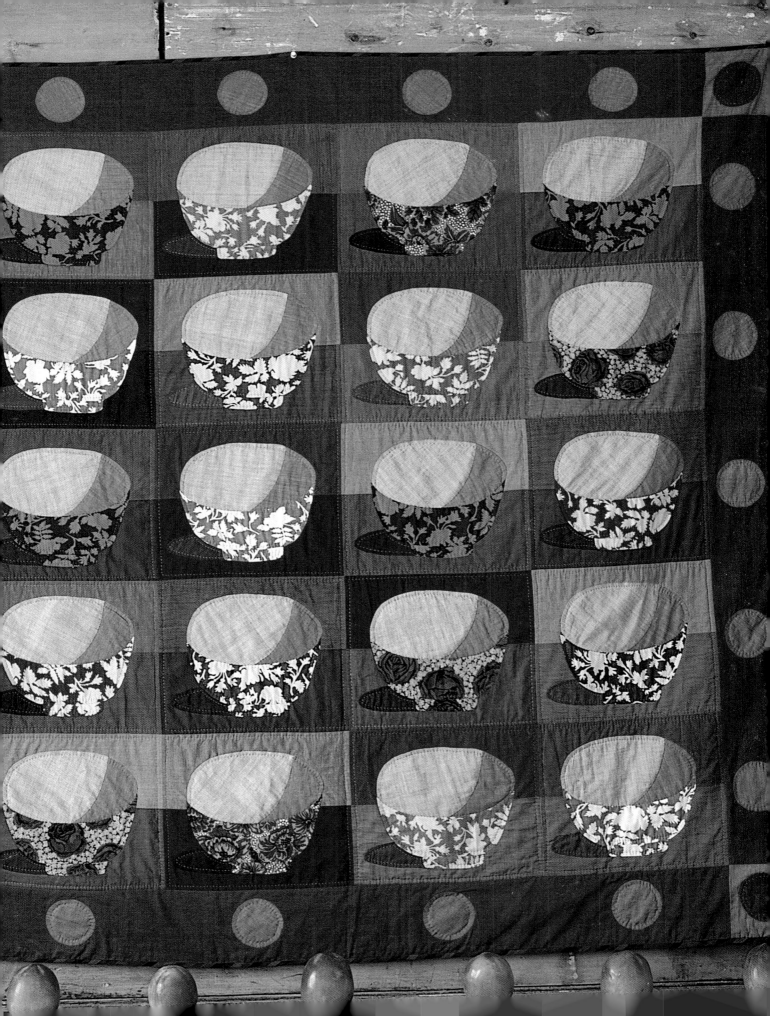

With all the sharp angles of the architectural world we inhabit, circles bring a soothing humanity. Think how a round window or arched doorway softens a hard-edge building. Patchworks using curves, like Wedding Ring quilts with interweaving striped circles, do the same while remaining dynamic. Another inspiration is the dramatic use of circles in traditional Persian suzani embroideries. One often sees gigantic star motifs in quilts, but rarely circles on this scale.

dark rice bowls

There is something about a simple bowl that makes me content. I have shelves full of bowls around my house and never tire of looking at them. The grouping of

bowls on the *Dark Rice Bowls* wall hanging (below left and previous page) was inspired by a painting I saw in Seattle. The repeat of the bowl with its pale interior and decorated sides has a pleasing rhythm. All of the fabrics in the patchwork are from my own quilt fabric collection (see page 159 for fabric information). My solid-coloured *Shot Cottons* in warm, earthy colours make a very livable palette, rather Tibetan in mood. The quilting is simple outline stitching done by hand around the bowl shapes, shadows and block patches.

Because blue-and-white seems to get more exciting to me each year, I based my alternative version of the *Dark Rice Bowls* around these colours. The bowls on the *Blue-and-White Rice Bowls* wall hanging (right) are cut from two of my

LEFT Hand-stitched appliqué and outline quilting give the *Dark Rice Bowls Hanging* a subtle and elegant texture. ABOVE The crisp shape of simple bowls features in many of my early and recent still lifes. RIGHT *Blue-and-White Rice Bowls* is made up of fewer bowls and includes sashing.

Pressed Roses prints. You could use different blue-and-white prints taken from your own scrap collection, but if you do, make sure they are crisp and simple. This will keep the quilt a calm influence in a room.

Mulling over other colourways for this bowls patchwork makes me think of a dish in my porcelain collection that is covered all over in pastel flowers. Imagine doing the *Rice Bowls* layout with all the pretty flower prints you could find – a different one in every single block. Or, for a more delicate mood, try French *toile de jouy* prints on pale grey grounds. If you don't fancy stitching such a large amount of appliqué, make a few cushions instead, each with a single bowl and with borders in a rich print.

pastel bubbles

Dots and spots have always attracted my designer's eye. Some time ago, while sitting in a Pennsylvania quilt shop doing a book signing with Liza, I was facing a wall of 1930's reproduction fabrics. They were really not my usual type of fabrics,

LEFT, ABOVE AND RIGHT A collection of 1930's reproduction quilt fabrics formed the basis for *Pastel Bubbles*, seen here (right) with Rupert Spira ceramics. Up close the prints appear rather cutsie (left), but they make a surprisingly sophisticated quilt. (See page 76 for instructions.)

but many had what I'd call 'dotty' themes that fascinated me – polka dots, little repeat roundish flowers, repeat circular-type leaves, and so on. Almost all of these prints were mostly white and had little

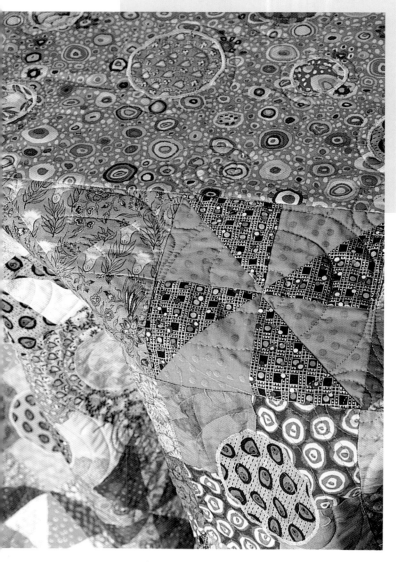

cutsie prints in sweet, soft and chalky pastel shades. They had a nostalgic character of fabrics found in old ladies' house dresses and aprons. Most of the time one sees them stitched into traditional pinwheel designs and Sunbonnet Sue appliqué patterns. By the time the book signing was over, I had

designed *Pastel Bubbles* in my head, and we left the shop with a stack of about thirty of these 1930's prints and a large batch of other, mostly white, fabrics.

Wanting to emphasize the joyous spottiness of most of the prints, I took out ones that were less dotty. Then I added to the collection a white fabric with fine pin dots that reads as grey at a distance. This became the field at the centre of the quilt on which to float a drift of various-size circles. Liza later used a contrasting pastel thread for the satin-stitch border around each of the circles (see page 18). The pinwheel border followed, with it's row of snowball blocks to echo the circles. Happily, the final effect is like a children's party or a wedding just as the couple walks through the confetti.

Liza wasn't so sure about the fabric selection for the *Pastel Bubbles* at first, but liked the final result and encouraged me to do a second colourway of this layout. The impression I get now when looking at my finished *Byzantine Bubbles* is quite different from the one I had when collecting the various fabrics for this version. The completed patchwork is so very earthy, in rich clay colours with brilliant stabs of jewel turquoise, lapis and cobalt accents. As one looks more deeply into it, softer muddy teals and dirtier turquoises emerge. There is a singing pale gold-yellow that also surfaces. The centre with my golden *Roman Glass* fabric works a treat with its tiny- and small-scale spots. After doing two colourways of the

FAR LEFT, LEFT AND BELOW
Byzantine Bubbles was made in exactly the same way as the *Pastel Bubbles* quilt on pages 18 and 19, but the alternative colour theme gives it a much richer, earthy look. The differing positions of the dark triangles on the pinwheel blocks makes them 'spin' in different directions and energizes the patchwork layout.

Bubbles patchwork myself, I just can't wait to see what readers come up with, since it is a design that could go on in so many directions. For instance, a very dark ground, even black, sprinkled with strong contrasting circles would be striking.

suzani quilt

Jack Francis, a textile expert who had a wonderful carpet shop in Piccadilly, London in the 70's, first introduced me to flamboyant embroidered suzani wall hangings. The way the Persian artisans played with circles of different scales on these antique textiles excited my imagination and led to knitting ideas like my *Persian Poppy*.

One comes across luscious embroidered suzani circles in so many different scales, often quite small red ones on a cream cloth surrounded by navy blue leaf-like details. Then suddenly, occasionally, one stumbles across a version with huge powerful circles – these thrill me to the bone. Although the circles are usually bright red embroideries on a cream ground, seeing other interesting colourways made me go for a golden scheme for my *Suzani Quilt*. It reminds me of the beaten brass trays my mother collected when I was a boy. I wanted a saturated golden ground with the orange and wine tones just rising to the surface. My Indian *Broad Stripe* fabric works well as the bias border to the solid circles, but you could use any similar multi-coloured stripe in its place.

The *Suzani Quilt* is one of the few designs in this book that I actually quilted by hand in my primitive running stitches. I used twisted embroidery thread in contrasting golds, reds and deep pink, and quilted irregular, wavy parallel lines across the circle appliqués and then the centre background, and concentric circles inside each snowball block.

The *Suzani* patchwork layout would be effective in any number of colourways – black and red for drama, or very stone-like colours for a soft, quiet interior. One design that I'm now dying to have a go at is to use the snowball blocks in the border

FAR LEFT, LEFT AND ABOVE This patchwork was named *Suzani Quilt* because it was inspired by antique Persian embroideries called suzanis. The patchwork blocks are all joined together, then the circles are appliquéd on top. (See page 80 for instructions). The quilt was photographed at Parham House in West Sussex. Notice my knitted cushion (far left), designed to echo the patchwork.

23

of the *Suzani Quilt* for an all-over pattern. It is amazing how the straight sides in the piecing of the snowballs give such a strong and convincing illusion of roundness. Viewed at a distance the quilt looks like circles surrounded by more circles.

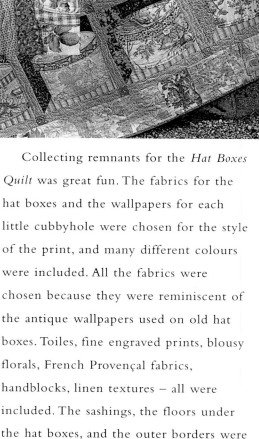

hat boxes quilt

I first got excited about hat boxes when I saw a collection of early ones at the American Museum in Bath in England. Bold-patterned wallpaper boxes in antique tones seemed a natural idea for a quilt. Liza had a great stash of French Provençal fabrics that worked wonderfully as deep wallpaper interiors for each cubbyhole. The trick with this design is to collect as many soft large-scale florals with quite light grounds as possible for the box and lid, and stripes and tight little repeat prints for the rim on each lid. The wallpapers should be fairly dense prints with almost no pale areas.

Collecting remnants for the *Hat Boxes Quilt* was great fun. The fabrics for the hat boxes and the wallpapers for each little cubbyhole were chosen for the style of the print, and many different colours were included. All the fabrics were chosen because they were reminiscent of the antique wallpapers used on old hat boxes. Toiles, fine engraved prints, blousy florals, French Provençal fabrics, handblocks, linen textures – all were included. The sashings, the floors under the hat boxes, and the outer borders were

ABOVE AND OPPOSITE PAGE The outer border toile fabrics on the *Hat Boxes Quilt* were soaked in a tea dye to give the backgrounds the same soft ecru hue. LEFT One tiny detail that helps make this project glow is the very bright scarlet red thread used to sew on the hat boxes.

all in soft beige with dusty colour accents, giving a consistent colour to glue together the huge variation of shades.

This project put to use a long-collected group of fabrics that came from the offcuts and remnants of fabulous interior decorating shops. Most of the hat boxes were cut from that treasured collection.

ninety degrees

As FAR BACK AS I can remember, I've been stopped in my tracks by arrangements of humble squares. Stacks of boxes on a shelf, bricks in a building yard, square-cut flint stone walls and aerial views of farmers' fields all make me remember how powerful this simplest of geometric forms can be. Because they are the easiest shapes to sew together, patchwork abounds in variations on the square. I never tire of flipping through books on old quilts, and there seems to be an endless flow of ideas based on nothing but this unaffected motif. Antique Dutch and English quilts especially contain fine, simple groupings of square patches.

RIGHT The large checkerboard blocks on the *Gypsy Garden* quilt are just strong enough to make themselves known without overshadowing the *Flower Lattice* print used for the large squares.
ABOVE, BOTTOM LEFT A collage of ripped magazine pages decorates a theatre door in Durban, South Africa.

A contemporary quilt that sticks in my mind is one of many small askew squares surrounded by a contrasting border of squares. It was such a basic format, yet people at the exhibition where I saw it kept coming back to this intriguing sheet of squares.

gypsy garden

The old chintz quilts have a bold, deeply intricate effect that is achieved by such amazingly simple patch arrangements. My *Gypsy Garden* was inspired by them. I started the design with big patches of a strong, large-scale print, and this is what gives such a lush impact. The crisp sixteen-patch checkerboard blocks float forward out of the dense print pattern. I was thinking of those dashing Spanish

TOP AND ABOVE *Gypsy Garden* and its alternative colourways are made up of simple square patches (See page 86 for instructions). OPPOSITE PAGE The *Spring Garden* version was pieced from all the leafiest of my own prints. If doing this with different prints, just keep everything madly fecund.

gypsy shawls of black silk embroidered with brilliant flowers when naming this quilt. My favourite part of the patchwork is the sumptuous antique bouquet fabric on the border – I had only just enough to complete it. This would make a very festive table cover for a party.

The simple geometry of the *Gypsy Garden* excited me so much that I designed three more versions of it, putting different colourways of my *Flower Lattice* fabric to the job it was designed

for. *Flower Lattice* is a very large-scale diaper pattern floral with a strong diagonal grid of tight leaves. Half the blocks in the *Gardens* are cut from this fabric, so its colour determines the mood and coloration of the checkerboards that are paired with it.

There is no mystery about the appeal of the tender green shades on the *Spring Garden* patchwork. Spring is that miracle time when with great awe we realize all over again that the world renews itself every year. The fresh pale greens here would turn a bedroom into an orangery! I could see this quilt singing out if placed against an oriental wallpaper with hand-painted plants on a duck-egg blue ground.

My *Ghost Garden* is built around the grey ('stone') colourway of the *Flower Lattice* print. I often joke about how one has to come to terms with grey to live in England, but I actually find grey palettes immensely appealing. There is something quite restful about their softness. Grey stones in a thousand shades on a beach can keep me staring for hours. Big Sur on the California coast is full of silvered wooden barns which always move me when I'm there visiting childhood haunts. Even my grey hair fascinates me as I peer

into the mirror wondering how it happened to me. The warm and cool shades of grey in *Ghost Garden* makes one think of old haunted houses.

What is it about the golden tones in the *Honey Garden* variation that is so soothing? Perhaps it is a reminder of glowing summer evenings. The dusky pinks, golden ochres and creams on the quilt are very warming, while the clear pale greens give a balancing cool element. To achieve the mood of this colour scheme you have to be careful not to break it with anything too dark or harshly bright.

The *Garden* quilt series is close to my heart, so I hope these four variations will show you the way to many original versions of your own.

LEFT AND ABOVE LEFT Touches of ochre and pink slightly warm the colour scheme in the *Ghost Garden* patchwork. ABOVE AND RIGHT *Honey Garden* with its soothing golden tones.

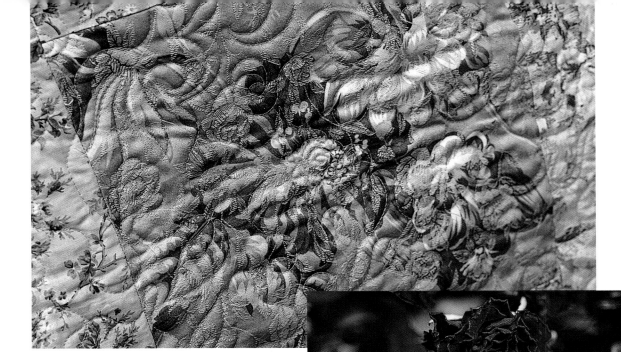

japanese brocades

The *Japanese Brocades* quilt is the result of my stumbling upon a great collection of Japanese brocades at the International Quilt Festival in Houston one year. Though they were a lot more expensive than the average patchwork fabric, Liza and I had to have them! Each fabric, with its large repeats, is so subtle and finely detailed that this simple layout of giant patches sprang to mind – the prints are just too gorgeous to cut into small pieces.

Because all the Japanese fabrics have a muted, antique quality, they harmonize together like a handsome stone wall. None of the flowers on their neutral grounds rises above a certain level, and many of the florals are printed on a damask ground which softens the total effect still further.

The inner border is cut from a print of roses on an eau-de-nil ground that is drawn to look like weaving or needlepoint. We then outlined the whole thing with a striped Chinese-robe-type border of all the brocades, and placed a 'fussy-cut' patch of my Designers Guild print *Rosamundi* at the border centres to feature its giant flowers on a lilac ground.

The cool blue sashing provides a contrast to these large warm squares, but the overall look is of a dipped-in-tea palette. I asked for a dense swirly quilting to further obscure the florals. In a cool, neutral room with bleached wood surfaces, this quilt would gently glow.

ABOVE AND RIGHT Liza and I bought a very expensive collection of Japanese brocaded rose prints and wanted to display their large repeats. The *Japanese Brocades* quilt with its simple squares of fabric surrounded by sashing was the result. (Instructions start on page 89.)

moody blues

I don't mind that the title of the *Moody Blues* quilt dates me – this pop group was one of my favourites when I came to England in the late 60's. For the patchwork, I gathered together groups of colours that would quietly contrast, so the overall effect would be a smear of blue with zingy magenta and gold accents pinging out. You could definitely make this quilt with more contrast between the blocks for a more sharply defined effect, while keeping the saturated blue theme going.

Years ago when I first moved to London, I painted only white-on-white still lifes. I was reminded of this restraint

ABOVE AND RIGHT The quilting stitches on *Moody Blues* effectively emphasize the diagonal bands of toned squares. LEFT AND TOP LEFT *Moody Whites* is a pale variation made from very subtle monochromatic prints in dusty, chalky colours.

when picking fabrics for an alternative colourway for the *Moody Blues,* which I called *Moody Whites.* Finding the right colours for this type of scheme was quite tricky to do successfully. I kept adding what appeared to be very pale fabrics that suddenly screamed out as though they were dayglow. If you're trying this yourself, my tip is just to collect as many variants as you can, choosing those that are so close in appearance you can barely tell them apart – and pale, pale, pale.

red courthouse steps

The *Red Courthouse Steps* is only my second attempt at log cabin patchwork – a design that often caught my eye in old quilt collections. It proves a very good vehicle for the saturated red colour story

I was after. I'm sure I'm not alone in being influenced by Matisse's *The Red Studio,* 1911, which I first saw as a young artist and was never able to forget. It's of a wonderful room painted brick red with all the furnishings in it the same warm colour. When you remove almost all other colour except vivid red tones you create excitement indeed. The rich red feathered robes of the Pacific island cultures spring to mind, as well as South American weaving and the red silk costumes of the Peking opera.

Shopping for all these saturated red fabrics for *Red Courthouse Steps* was thrilling, and once they were sewn

LEFT, ABOVE AND RIGHT *Red Courthouse Steps* became the first of three versions of this log cabin patchwork format. Pictured right with my knitted *Courthouse Cushion.* (See page 96 for instructions for making the quilt.)

together the result was more than I had hoped for – great and small prints cut up so deliciously! The deep wine-reds set off the hot magentas and blood-orange tones beautifully, and the scattering of greens and golds on the prints vitalizes the palette. Don't make the same mistake I did by adding in anything with too much white in it. I had incorporated a gorgeous white rose print with a deep claret ground, but found it jumped out terribly from the finished arrangement. To remedy this I painted magenta dye over the white rose areas and they settled into the general scarletness. My own red *Roman Glass* print provided a sympathetic

border, while the chartreuse squares at the centre of the blocks are delicately radiant.

Gathering the many shades of yellow fabric for *Yellow Courthouse Steps* was like picking yellow flowers in a wild meadow! I tried to stick to solids and very dense yellow-on-yellow prints. Though the occasional fabric had some pale blue or some pink and cream, any print with a lot of white was eliminated – the whites made the look too soft. I used deep golds, lemons and paler primrose yellows, but a saturated look was called for, so I tried to resist any borderline prints that would get too pink or blue and dilute the story. It looks like lemons,

OPPOSITE PAGE Embroidery was used on the *Yellow Courthouse Steps* to tone down the chartreuse centre squares. THIS PAGE *Indigo Courthouse Steps* contains Japanese, Indonesian and African indigo prints.

bananas and papaya, don't you think?

Once the fabrics were gathered, cut into strips and sewn around a central chartreuse square, I was shocked to see how dark and hard the centres appeared. The same chartreuse used on the other two *Courthouse Steps* looked really bright. It seems the dazzling bright yellow had turned what looked chartreuse on its own into dark, muddy moss. My solution was to use this green as the centres of dozens of embroidered 'daisies'. Once I got into it, playing with the concentric rings of colour in each flower was quite fun. At the centre of the flowers I left a small circle of chartreuse fabric visible, which

became a better accent than the original dead square. The flowers are all done in simple radiating straight stitches, started in the middle of the daisy. I used some silk thread and a lot of knitting and embroidery cottons, all in a high oriental palette. The threads in bright pinks, sky blues and apple greens are a good contrast to the many shades of yellow. Tiny seed stitches in the chartreuse centres and little orange star stitches 'tie' the quilt together.

How different the *Indigo Courthouse Steps* version of this quilt is from its red cousin, even though the blocks share the same chartreuse centre squares (see page 39). When travelling in South Africa I was struck by the great variety in native indigo prints. They are everywhere in that most fascinating country – brought in by the Dutch probably. I used to rack my brains to think how they could be used effectively. This log cabin variation seemed suddenly just right. We added in patches from Liza's own collection of

Japanese, Indonesian and African indigo prints. It was stimulating playing with the amazing variety in such a restricted palette. Large prints appear lighter, while the tiny dots and checks give a deep blue effect. It's hard to believe that only indigo is used here, because so many shades and densities emerge. And despite all the very dark blue grounds on the prints, the quilt is surprisingly lively and light.

nona

The year before my grandmother died she gave me a gorgeous Middle Eastern embroidery of rich pink, yellows, limes and black silk geometry. Before I could properly enjoy it, it was stolen from me, but the memory had burnt into my mind. So thirty years later I have made an attempt at recreating it in patchwork. The strongest enduring impression was the brilliant clash of sunny yellows and candy

LEFT AND RIGHT Adding blue and ecru striped sashing to the *Nona* quilt calmed the sunny yellows, candy pinks and lavenders in the freeform log cabin blocks. (See page 99 for instructions.)

pinks with the lime. In my *Nona* quilt, I used these strong colours and added lavenders in the form of warm clear lilacs through to deeper, cooler tones.

When choosing fabrics for your rendition of *Nona*, keep the palette high and clear, and include only a couple of dustier antique notes, such as grey-blue or wine. The striped dusty blue and ecru sashing and border, which look like mattress ticking, calm the hot pastels giving that old-fashioned feel I am so attracted to! Each block is quilted with a big squared-off spiral starting at the centre of each block, and the sashing and border with four freeform parallel lines.

blocks look like charming framed squares. The background behind the slightly askew solid centre squares is cut away so that the light can glow through.

In time, washing the *Squares Window Blind* will gently fray the raw edges of the centre squares, which is meant to be part of the unkempt charm of the design.

squares window blind

In a book on Russian interiors I noticed that someone had used an unbacked piece of patchwork as a lampshade to great effect. Wanting to do a soft window blind in the same way, I picked faded pastel and white-toned fabrics. To create a checkerboard, blocks of pale prints were alternated with light- to medium-toned ones. Fabrics in the paler group were chosen because they are reminiscent of soft blue transferware and fussy flowery china dishes – mostly blue-and-white-teacup sort of prints. For the opposing blocks we used all the various shades of coloured chalks. The addition of a gauzy raw-edged square of light putty or pale peach on top of each square gives the window blind the appearance of layers of squares upon squares, and the individual

LEFT AND ABOVE Instead of picking faded pastel and white-toned fabrics like this for your *Squares Window Blind*, you could really get dramatic with all reds perhaps, or you might prefer many shades of pink – with pale apple green centres they would give a soft, warm light to a room.

angled delights

ONCE WE HAVE seen how imaginative arrangements of simple squares can be, slicing one diagonally to form a triangle gives us a whole new element to play with in patchwork. But the angled patch that sends our design possibilities into orbit is the basic diamond. Even straight rows of diamonds are quite jazzy, but elegant tumbling blocks and compelling stars flow easily from this pointy shape. This chapter is full of triangles, diamonds and stars, and includes designs with energetic pinwheel blocks and one with a simple allover zigzag pattern (see page 57). My head spins at the staggering use of stars in old quilts. As elements in borders or allover repeats, large and

RIGHT The rusts, ochres, moss greens, turquoise and cobalt accents of the *Fonthill Quilt* colour scheme were inspired by Henry Mercer's 'castle' in Doylestown, Pennsylvania. The meandering machine-quilted lichen shapes temper the energetic geometric pinwheels. (See page 105 for instructions.)

small, they are impressive; but most dramatic of all are those with one mammoth star covering the entire quilt. Sometimes these huge single stars are made up of many diamonds or done with great vigour as string diamonds, which are striped at random with scrap fabrics (see page 10).

fonthill quilt

In my first book on patchwork, a magical museum became the photography location for some of my quilts. It was Liza who first took me to visit Fonthill. It is an eccentric Arts and Craft's 'castle' built by Henry Mercer in Doylestown, Pennsylvania. The building is one of the earliest in cast concrete and is studded everywhere with Mercer's huge and impressive collection of antique and purpose-made tiles. It has the quality of a sandy desert embedded with gems.

I was so haunted by the beauty of these very original interiors, but was struck by the lack of appropriate textiles to go with the earthy palette of the tiles. This led me to dream up a patchwork quilt that would reflect the interiors and

ABOVE LEFT The tonal contrast on the pinwheel fabrics is so subtle in many places on the *Fonthill Quilt* that the pinwheels barely 'spin'. LEFT, ABOVE AND RIGHT *Haitian Fonthill* uses the same layout, but a completely different colour scheme.

their Byzantine arches encrusted with high glazes that harmonize so well with the stones and concrete of the building. The *Fonthill Quilt,* with its rusts, ochres, moss greens, turquoise and cobalt accents, is very like my memories of Mercer's castle. It also reminds me of dried flowers dropped in the mud.

One of Liza's passions in life is collecting Haitian primitive paintings. I, too, like the high pastel colours of some of these densely detailed landscapes. Many are pure fantasies of apple green hills, pink trees and dayglow turquoise skies. Taking all the brilliant magentas, sky blues, apple greens and turquoises I could find, I worked out a totally different version of mossy old *Fonthill* and called it *Haitian Fonthill* (see page 47).

Instead of the earthy tile colours of the original, I played with the dazzling pastels of a Haitian colour scheme. The result, because of the fractured nature of the piecing, is actually not as garishly bright as you might imagine. I think we end up with a very liveable bed cover charged with optimistic hues – rather like a big tray of broken blackboard chalks.

If you're looking for an interior to put *Haitian Fonthill* in, it would be a cool surprise in a soft yellow or pink room. The ambitious might like to try changing the wide borders done in my *Gazania* print – the whole mood could be transformed just by using a different fabric for these. (See page 109 for instructions for *Haitian Fonthill*.)

wedding quilt

I don't know about you, but I've always been deeply moved by old stripped-down walls with fragments of past wallpapers scattered about them. With this in mind, I began my star-studded *Wedding Quilt* by picking an array of the palest prints I could lay my hands on. They appeared next door to white, yet when they were sewn together I was amazed how distinct some of them became. There are no really

THIS PAGE AND NEXT PAGE The *Wedding Quilt* is a *tour de force* of gentle, faded tones. The patches are cut from an assortment of prints, florals and stripes. (See page 110 for diagrams and instructions.)

sharp prints in this fabric assortment –
instead there are monochromatic prints,
washed-out toiles, stripes, very muted
old-fashioned florals and some plaids. The
patchwork appears to have been washed
and faded in the sunlight for decades!
And the allover effect is a sweet
confection that definitely reminds me of
all the wallpaper bits still stuck to the
walls in those half-stripped rooms.

This starry arrangement is a mixture
of star blocks and pinwheel blocks

surrounded by a zigzag border – all the pointy shapes give the geometry amazing movement, which contrasts boldy with the subdued colouring. The entire patchwork is covered with a gentle machine-quilted floral-shaped repeat that blends in well with the predominant floral prints.

The *Wedding Quilt* would look so different if done with crisper contrasts – charcoal greys with chalky deep pastel prints for instance. It's up to you to go there, but I may beat you to it!

delft baskets

For many years I've been leafing through books on antique quilts and stopping abruptly at a pattern that lends itself to knitting design – 'Lady of the Lake'. I used it in my summer 1998 Rowan knits collection, and it knitted up like a dream.

As I was preparing material for this book, the same old quilt caught my eye, and this simplified version, the *Delft Baskets* tablecloth, grew out of it.

Loving blue and white as I do, I was interested to find a new layout that would suit my *Pressed Roses* fabric prints. They became half of the big square blocks made up of two large triangles and set 'on point' in the checkerboard ground. These blocks ended up looking like baskets of roses, so that is what I called the design. The inky deep blue 'basket' fabrics were chosen for their colour and because they each suggested a woven-basket texture.

LEFT, ABOVE AND RIGHT The *Delft Baskets* colour scheme came out of my passion for blue and white, a passion evident in my large collection of blue-and-white ceramics. (See page 113 for instructions for making *Delft Baskets*.)

The rough country feel of the prints and weaves of the dark baskets works well with the dusty palette of the blue-and-white surrounding squares. In the end the composition reminds me of Japanese peasant farmers' patched jackets.

Mosses in the autumn must have been on my mind as I put together the colours for the alternative colourway of the *Delft Baskets,* which I called *Citrus Baskets Throw*. All the fabrics for this version came from my own collection. The dusky ochres and oranges of my solid-coloured *Shot Cottons* make an earthy ground for the rich Indian woven stripes and the golds and yellows in my range of prints. I love the sparks of magenta and burnt oranges, and the brilliant greens flicker out of this toasty arrangement like jewels.

Meandering machine-quilted squiggles unify the checkerboard ground on both versions of the *Baskets*. But the basket blocks seemed to need individual treatment – slanting lines were used on these on *Delft Baskets*, while on *Citrus Baskets* flower shapes cover the 'flowers' and parallel lines the striped 'baskets'.

THIS PAGE AND NEXT PAGE The patches for the *Citrus Baskets Throw* were all cut from my own quilt fabrics (see page 159). My fabrics play a minor role in many of my patchwork designs because they provide just the colour I'm looking for, or form the perfect border or binding, but in a few quilts they provide a whole glorious palette.

pink flags

Every once in a while, one wants a bold celebratory layout that will signal optimism in this serious world. The Japanese at times use a singingly high pastel palette that makes me as happy as a child's innocent laughter does. It puts one in mind of birthday cakes or flower-covered floats in a parade. I used this colour mood for my *Pink Flags* quilt. The starting point was the pink colourway of my *Roman Glass* print, and it became the base for the design, featuring in the extra-large triangles. I then gathered together all the bright multi-coloured and monochromatic prints I could find. The aim was to have a pink element in most of the large pieced-diamonds flag shapes so that they would partly fade into the background. I'm particularly happy with

the striking acid lime shots and the bold red-and-white stripes going off at so many different angles. A few patches of my *Pressed Roses* in red as well as in gold found a happy home here. The delicious sky blues in the quilt make for cool zinging notes. You could hang this on a front porch on any celebration day.

I'd love to see the *Pink Flags* arrangement done in dark brights as well. It would be fun to choose another of my *Roman Glass* colourways for the large background triangles, pull the accent shades out of it for the diamond patches and make a totally different *Flags* quilt.

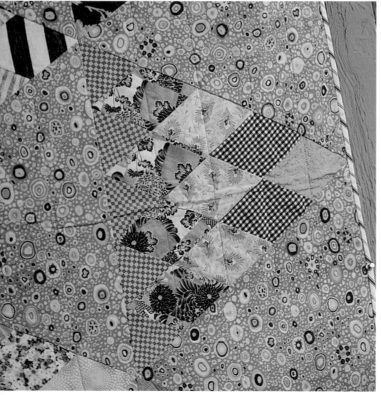

LEFT, ABOVE AND RIGHT The severity of the straight parallel quilting lines on the *Pink Flags* patchwork provides a good contrast on this frivolous quilt. It looks at home on this beach hut. (See page 116 for instructions.)

RIGHT AND BELOW A happy, cheerful table topper, the *Pinwheel Tablecloth* is pictured here with my 'patchwork' mosaic pot. OPPOSITE PAGE The appliquéd jars on *Ginger Jars* sometimes appear to jump forwards and at other times recede. (See instructions for on pages 119 and 121.)

pinwheel tablecloth

What is it about the simple patchwork pinwheel that is so delightful? Perhaps it is the childhood memory of paper or bright plastic pinwheels at the circus. They signal a lightness of spirit and can add movement to any quilt border. On the *Pinwheel Tablecloth,* the whole patchwork dances with the playful shapes and their relentless contrasts.

The colour scheme was inspired by the wonderful Tibetan patchworks I've seen with dusky, slightly faded jewel-coloured brocades. My solid-coloured

Shot Cotton fabrics have just the earthy, tempered brightness I was looking for. Most of the assorted fabrics used are monochromatic prints that appear solid at a distance, but the odd obvious print occasionally breaks up the triangles and adds to the complex look of the simple geometry.

If you like the warmth of this particular balance of colours, be careful not to get too harshly bright in your choices. The colours are combined so that each individual pinwheel has two fairly contrasty fabrics. But a few of the pinwheels have a 'mistake' patch which makes one of the blades quite different from the other three. This keeps the patchwork pattern unpredictable and gives it a whimsical feel.

ginger jars

Anyone who knows my previous books will have spotted my attraction to oriental pots as a theme. The way Indians, Chinese, Indonesians and Japanese use pot shapes

in architecture and textiles always lights me up. When I went to visit a wonderful pink dining room in a great English country house, the idea for this pink and red *Ginger Jars* quilt popped into my mind. The allover mood is definitely pink and red. My *Pressed Roses* print, used for the ginger jars, looks to my eye like one of those densely detailed oriental jars. The background is made up of sweet, cool pinks and contrasting maroons and deep magentas, and the border introduces

a shot of lively aqua and deep clear magenta with vivid moss or apple green. With the darker dead plum *Pressed Rose* as the outer border, these shades feel almost Chinese.

A bold idea like this lends itself to many colour moods, and I look forward to playing further with it and to seeing what you come up with. Just to get you going, here is a suggestion: for a really exciting spring quilt, try mad flower prints in a riot of pastels, with solids in apple greens contrasted with pale peaches and creams in the zigzag background! You could also forget the ginger jars altogether — I actually think simple planes of zigzags like this in contrast colours would make a very graphic quilt.

stripes galore

I CAN'T THINK of any culture, or any time in history, where stripes have not played a big part in decoration. Japanese kabuki curtains with their broad bands of rich colours, striped china, striped weaves on Scandinavian national costumes, and crocheted stripes on African dance outfits are just a few of the visions that flow vividly through my mind. Then there are mown fields, pebbled walkways, British flags painted on football fans' faces – the list is endless and rich in contrasts. There is much there to spark off ideas for using stripes in patchwork. Striped borders and edges have long been a feature in my quilt designs, but for this chapter, I have designed a series of quilts that are covered with lively arrangements of striped fabrics.

RIGHT The vibrant stripes on my *Handkerchief Corners* are from a range of striped fabrics that I designed for a village of weavers in India – at the request of the international charity Oxfam. They have since been used by patchworkers all over the world. (See page 124 for instructions and diagrams for this quilt.) My favourite stripes are on the enamel colander above.

is certainly one for the 'colour players' of this world – can't wait to see the variations.

The palette on my version utilizes my collection of handwoven stripes made in India. I used the entire range except for the palest pastel colourways. The overall effect is smoldering earthy, autumnal colours, with sparks of jewel magentas, turquoises, lavenders and blue throughout. We were going to use just one size block, but when I visited Liza's studio I found the offcuts of the larger blocks so charming that I made her do a panel of them in the centre of the quilt. The quilting in-the-

ABOVE AND RIGHT You can give *Handkerchief Corners* a different appearance just by changing the colour of the little squares in the large blocks. OPPOSITE PAGE The *Optical Squares Tablecloth* is a perfect project for using up scraps of stripes. (See page 128 for instructions.)

handkerchief corners

I first saw the *Handkerchief Corners* geometric design on a stunning American rag rug, but have since seen it everywhere! It's in tiles, mosaic, and dozens of knit designs, especially those brilliantly done by German designer Horst Schultz, who has made a whole career on this one pattern. It's another of those great layouts that is so stunningly simple you can't stop looking at it. The large squares are traditional Attic Window blocks. This quilt

optical squares

After dreaming up the *Bright Optical Squares Cushion* on page 66, I felt the urge to experiment with scales on this simple yet complex-looking design. I put together my Indian stripe fabrics however they fell, which led to all sorts of delightful variations on the same square format. The appearance of red/maroon with ochre notes is quite deliberate. You can see what a rich tablecloth *Optical Squares* makes. Imagine it on a Christmas table with bowls of pomegranates, oranges and plums, and deep red candles.

Because the striped triangles that make each block don't need to match, this is

ditch emphasizes the diagonals and turns the blocks into peacock feathers.

The wonderful thing about my multi-coloured stripes fabric collection is that the striped patches can look very different depending on which colour bands are used. If you want to make this quilt with a redder or bluer slant, just choose and cut the Indian stripes to bring out that bias.

RIGHT AND FAR RIGHT We bought new shirting fabrics for our *Shirt-Stripe Boxes*, but it would be fun to make it from real shirts that are on their way to secondhand shops. (See page 130 for instructions.) BELOW This cushion is a new colourway of a design in my first patchwork book. Its striped squares are made from patches rather than striped fabrics.

shirt-stripe boxes

When I arrived in England in the 60's, I was turned on by the enormous variety of men's shirting fabrics in the windows of men's tailors. It was only a matter of time before I put them into a design. Most of the fabrics used in *Shirt-Stripe Boxes* come from the same little shop off Berwick Street in London. It was a joyous day's shopping, picking out all the bolts of gorgeous Sea Island cottons in bold and fine stripes. Though not all the stripes included in the quilt are purely blue and white – there are some reds and greys – the overall look is of blue and white. The restraint of the colours emphasizes the frisky variations in block scale.

In-the-ditch quilting in the diagonal seams of the patchwork softens the

the perfect project to use up all those stripe scraps left over from other projects. We selected leftover scraps of my stripes, keeping purple and plum as the dominant theme. You really can't go wrong with any stripes for this project. Printed or woven stripes; small-, medium- or large-scale stripes; thin or fat stripes, all will work. The stripes on the four triangles in each block aren't supposed to line up at all, which makes this an easy quilt to sew.

squareness of the patches, especially where you get a series of diagonals lining up over several blocks.

As you can see from the foundation-pieced cushion on page 62, this concentric squares idea begs to be translated into many colour moods. Done larger scale with furnishing fabrics, it would make exciting drapes or couch covers.

stars and stripes

There is something indomitable in most Americans' spirits that makes them love to dance on the table from time to time. The bold stripes and checks rising up out of the old reproduction print background on the *Stars and Stripes* quilt are a case in point. Wisely, the old paisley-like print tempers the brashness of the outspoken stars.

When I first proudly showed this design in Germany, one viewer screamed 'my God, it's hideous!' It's a dynamic layout at any rate. The patchwork format came from an old Texas Star quilt top I found at the International Quilt Festival in Houston one year. I've done another version of this with my *Chard* prints – very kaleidoscopic on my grey *Roman Glass* print.

The quilting on *Stars and Stripes* was my very first attempt at hand quilting. Inspired by the primitive bold stitches on Indian quilts, I used cotton knitting yarns in contrasting colours to make the stitches really show up. Using shades of reds to stitch the blue stars and shades of

BELOW AND RIGHT *Stars and Stripes* is a challenging quilt to make; there are lots of inset seams to deal with. But it's a worthwhile project if you want a layout with impact. (Instructions start on page 132.)

blues to stitch the burgundy stars, I started in the centre of each star and spiralled out to the points.

Try your own variation on this bold geometry. My suggestion would be a version with solid stars cut from my *Shot Cottons* on a ground of my *Damask* print – it could be quite intense.

optical squares cushions

Mixing triangles of woven Guatemalan stripes, printed Christmas stripes and other hot, bright fabrics was like making collages with gift wrapping paper – amusing and zany with not too much concern for good taste! If you are making the *Bright Optical Squares Cushion*, to achieve the same effect keep to bold contrasts in loud jewel-bright tones, with only the occasional cream note for extra contrast. Flame turquoise blue is great for sparking off the crimson and greens, and shocking deep orange is another enriching note.

My alternative colourway, *Pastel Optical Squares Cushion*, was joyous to assemble. I chose fabrics in colours

OPPOSITE PAGE The way the stripes meet on the *Bright Optical Squares Cushion* (top) and the pastel alternative (bottom) is purposely accidental. Unmatched stripes are enticingly fresh and edgy. LEFT Make your own stripes with fabric strips for this *Turban Footstool* patchwork. (See pages 135 and 136 for instructions.)

inspired by 50's Miami décor, cut them into triangle patches all the same size and played for an afternoon. The fabrics used are mostly bits of stripes in chalky dull rose pinks and pastel blues.

turban footstool

Wasn't the design of the *Turban Footstool* an idea just waiting to happen? When you experiment with strip patches there is no end to it, and this gathering of rich bands of pattern into a circular shape makes such a witty number. The inspiration came from a wonderful shop in New York called MacKenzie Childs, where everything is deliciously crammed with pattern and colour. They did a stool something like

this in plaid ties if I remember rightly.

The palette on my footstool would suit dark oriental carpets or red velvet over-stuffed chairs. The colours are arranged so that some of the fabrics flow subtly from one to another and others are starkly different from the neighbouring ones. A good rule of thumb is to place two or three strips that blend smoothly and then add in one abrupt change.

Stripes of contrasting fabrics in the *Turban Footstool* opens the mind to many possibilities. You could try it in pastels or the colours of the *Red Courthouse Steps* on page 37. Shirts, waistcoats or simple cushions of radiating stripes like this would make rich designs.

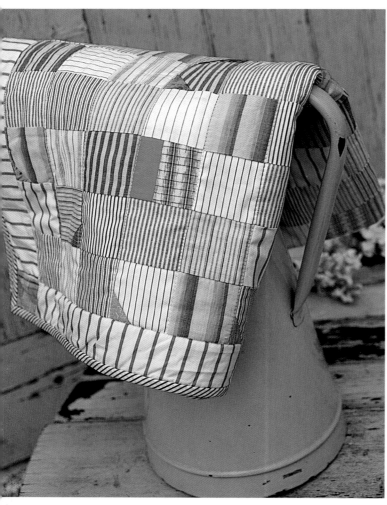

baby's corrugated quilt

I was trying to get with the minimal restrained brigade and the result made me think of corrugated metal panels – hence the name. In Australia and New Zealand they use this corrugated metal for many things; one artist even made a car covered in rusty corrugated tin. There's an idea! Try the quilt in browns, golds and greys for the more sophisticated baby – and it wouldn't show stains as easily. Or the colours of the *Bright Optical Cushion* would give this idea a rich twist (see page 66).

The vibration caused when several varying stripes are placed together is fascinating. I remember being dazzled by stacked bolts of shirt stripings in bespoke shirtmakers shops when I first got to England. It took me thirty years, but here is a design that occurred to me then.

Even brand new, this quilt appears well worn and loved. The colours are soft blues or grey-blues on white or ecru grounds, and tiny accents of hot pastels. The pastel fragments are meant to zing out, so the fresher and brighter the better.

THIS PAGE AND NEXT PAGE Most of the fabrics in the *Baby's Corrugated Quilt* are men's shirting fabrics. The tiny tabs of accent colours were pulled out of our now copious scrap bag.

FAR LEFT, LEFT AND BELOW Pale shades were used to create a quiet pastel mood on the *African Weave Throw*, but imagine this patchwork made in deep earth tones that are closer to an actual African palette. (See page 140 for instructions.)

african weave throw

My friend Peter Adler, who collects and writes books about art and textiles, first alerted me to the wonderful world of inventive African design. I now pore over books on Kuba textile geometrics, astounded at the huge and diverse array of dark and light shapes, mostly done in an ochre-straw colour and a peat brown. My *African Weave Throw* patchwork is just one of the spin-offs of this obsession.

My idea was to create a light, airy quilt for a spare, modern room. As the base, I used my collection of *Ombré Stripe* fabrics – all with pale ecru grounds and soft colours – and my *Blue and White Stripes*, which resemble mattress ticking or well-worn kitchen towels. The *Ombré Stripe* patches form a light 'woven' grid, which is punctuated with solid colours of my deeper *Shot Cottons*. The striped squares that make up the 'woven' grid are cut without regard to matching the stripes, and are just sewn together as they come. The unaligned stripes give the whole thing a wonderful primitive-weave feel.

making the patchworks

DETAILED instructions follow for all the main patchworks shown at the beginning of the book. Diagrams for piecing and assembly are included.

Some of the main patchworks have been made in another colourway, and colour descriptions for the alternative fabrics are provided, although separate instructions are not given for these.

Templates for the patchworks are given on pages 150–157.

Before beginning a patchwork, read all of the instructions – this will give you an idea of what techniques are involved and the level of experience required. Patchworks with inset seams and those with appliqué are not recommended for absolute beginners.

All the basic patchwork techniques are given on pages 143–149, so if you are a beginner, you should read these instructions first.

dark rice bowls hanging

The instructions that follow are for the *Dark Rice Bowls* wall hanging. The entire patchwork is made from KAFFE FASSETT fabrics. If you are using other fabrics, select similar warm, earthy tones. For experienced patchworkers, fabric colour descriptions for making the alternative colourway called *Blue-and-White Rice Bowls Hanging* are given on page 76.

SIZE
The finished *Dark Rice Bowls* measures approximately 55in × 56½in (140cm × 143.5cm).
Note that measurements on the diagrams are for finished patch sizes, excluding the seam allowances.

Special note: The blocks in this quilt are made from two simple rectangles pieced together in the usual way. A bowl and its shadow are appliqued on to each pieced blocked before the blocks are assembled into a top.

INGREDIENTS
45in (114cm) wide 100% cotton KAFFE FASSETT *quilt fabrics (see page 159 for fabric information):*
• **Fabric A (walls, floors and floor shadows):** ½yd (46cm) each of *Shot Cotton* in 'raspberry' (SC08), 'pomegranate' (SC09), 'tobacco' (SC18) and 'smoky' (SC20),or four similar solid-coloured fabrics in raspberry red, pomegranate red, tobacco brown and grey-blue; ¼yd (25cm) each of *Shot Cotton* in 'ginger' (SC01), 'cassis' (SC02), 'prune' (SC03), 'slate' (SC04), 'bittersweet' (SC10), 'chartreuse' (SC12), 'navy' (SC13), 'lavender' (SC14), 'pewter' (SC22) and 'charcoal' (SC25) or 10 similar solid-coloured fabrics in ginger, deep wine red, deep purple, dark brown-blue, dusty orange, deep chartreuse, navy, lavender, deep brown and charcoal
• **Fabric B (inside-bowl appliqué):** ¾yd (70cm) of 'duck egg' *Shot Cotton* (SC26) or a similar solid-coloured duck-egg blue fabric
• **Fabric C (inside-bowl shadow appliqué, etc.):** ¾yd (70cm) of 'opal' *Shot Cotton* (SC05) or a similar solid-coloured lavender-blue fabric
• **Fabric D (bowl appliqué):** ¼yd (25cm) each of *Pressed Rose* in five colourways (PR01, PR02, PR04, PR05 and PR06), or five similar bicolour prints – one with off-white flowers on a grey ground, one with yellow flowers on a dark gold ground, one with light salmon flowers on a deep plum ground, one with white flowers on a dark green ground and one with cream flowers on a coral red ground; plus ¼yd (25cm) each of *Damask* (GP02-J) or a similar medium-scale print of red and pink flowers on an olive ground with white dots, and *Forget-Me-Not Rose* (GP08-J) or a similar medium-scale print of red roses on a gold ground
• **Fabric E (border strips, etc.):** 1¾yd (1.6m) of 'persimmon' *Shot Cotton* (SC07) or a similar solid-coloured orange-red fabric
• **Backing fabric:** 3½yd (3.2m)
• **Binding fabric:** ¾yd (70cm) of *Narrow Stripe* (NS17) or a similar multi-coloured stripe in mostly dark magentas and reds
• **Lightweight cotton batting:** 62in × 64in (158cm × 162cm)
• **Quilting thread:** Greyish lavender thread
• **Templates and appliqués:** Use templates PP, QQ and RR, and appliqué shapes on pages 150 and 154, enlarging them as instructed

MAKING APPLIQUÉ TEMPLATES

Trace each of the five appliqué shapes separately on to a piece of paper, then add a ¼in (6mm) hem allowance around each shape and cut out the paper templates. (If you want a stiff template, glue each shape to a piece of cardboard and cut out.)

CUTTING PATCHES

Cut the pieces for the border before cutting the other patches so you can use some of the remaining fabrics for the quilt-centre patches.

Border

22 border circles: Cut 18 template-RR circles from fabric C ('opal') and four from fabric E ('persimmon').

4 border strips: From fabric E ('persimmon'), cut two strips 5in × 48in (13cm × 122cm) and two strips 5in × 46½in (13cm × 118cm).

4 border corners: Cut four 5in × 5in (13cm × 13cm) squares from fabric C.

Quilt centre

Use the templates on page 154 for the following:

20 'wall' rectangles: Cut one template-PP rectangle for each of the 20 blocks from A fabrics – four 'lavender'; three each 'ginger', 'raspberry' and 'chartreuse'; two each 'persimmon', 'pomegranate' and 'tobacco'; and one 'bittersweet'.

20 'floor' rectangles: Cut one template-QQ rectangle for each of the 20 blocks from A fabrics – three each 'prune', 'raspberry', 'pomegranate', 'tobacco' and 'smoky'; two each 'slate'

and 'pewter'; and one 'cassis'.
Use the appliqué templates to cut the following pieces:

20 floor-shadow appliqués: Cut 20 inside-bowl appliqués from A fabrics – six 'navy'; four each 'prune' and 'pewter'; three 'cassis'; two 'charcoal'; and one 'pomegranate'.

20 inside-bowl appliqués: Cut 20 inside-bowl appliqués from fabric B ('duck egg').

20 inside-bowl shadow appliqués: Cut 20 inside-bowl appliqués from fabric C ('opal').

20 bowl appliqués: Cut 20 bowl appliqués (and matching bowl bases) from fabric D – four *Pressed Rose*-PR04 (plum ground); three each *Pressed Rose*-PR01 (grey ground), *Pressed Rose*-PR02 (gold ground), *Pressed Rose*-PR05 (green ground) and *Forget-Me-Not Rose*-GP08-J; and two

each *Pressed Rose*-PR06 (coral red ground) and *Damask*-GP02-J.

BLOCK COLOURS

Each large block in the quilt centre is made from a 'wall' rectangle and a 'floor' rectangle. Then a bowl and its shadow are appliquéd on to the pieced blocks.

Before stitching the blocks together and sewing on the appliqué pieces, organize the patches needed for each block. The inside-bowl and inside-bowl shadow appliqués are the same on all the blocks, but the other colours vary.

Large block

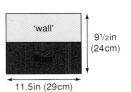

'wall'

'floor'

9½in (24cm)

11.5in (29cm)

TEMPLATES

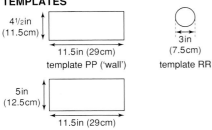

4½in (11.5cm)

11.5in (29cm)

template PP ('wall')

3in (7.5cm)

template RR

5in (12.5cm)

11.5in (29cm)

template QQ ('floor')

ASSEMBLY

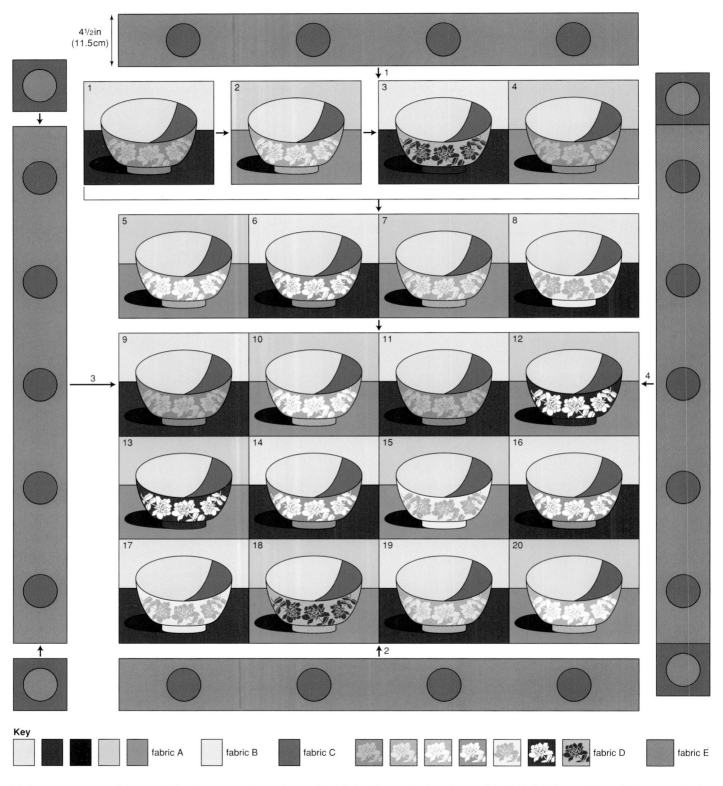

4½in
(11.5cm)

Key

fabric A   fabric B   fabric C   fabric D   fabric E

Make your own colour combinations by trying different arrangements with the cut patches and appliqué pieces, making sure that the floor is darker than the wall and the floor shadow is darker than the floor. Alternatively, follow the combinations used on the quilt pictured, which are as follows:

Block 1: Wall 'raspberry', floor 'smoky', bowl and base *Pressed Rose*-PR04 (plum), floor shadow 'navy'.
Block 2: Wall 'ginger', floor

'pomegranate', bowl and base *Pressed Rose*-PR02 (gold), floor shadow 'prune'.

Block 3: Wall 'tobacco', floor 'raspberry', bowl and base *Damask*-GP02-J, floor shadow 'cassis'.

Block 4: Wall 'lavender', floor 'pewter', bowl and base *Pressed Rose*-PR04 (plum), floor shadow 'charcoal'.

Block 5: Wall 'pomegranate', floor 'cassis', bowl and base *Pressed Rose*-PR01 (grey), floor shadow 'prune'.

Block 6: Wall 'chartreuse', floor 'slate', bowl and base *Pressed Rose*-PR05 (green), floor shadow 'pewter'.

Block 7: Wall 'bittersweet', floor 'tobacco', bowl and base *Pressed Rose*-PR02 (gold), floor shadow 'pewter'.

Block 8: Wall 'chartreuse', floor 'smoky', bowl and base *Forget-Me-Not Rose*-GP08-J, floor shadow 'navy'.

Block 9: Wall 'raspberry', floor 'smoky', bowl and base *Pressed Rose*-PR04 (plum), floor shadow 'navy'.

Block 10: Wall 'persimmon', floor 'pomegranate', bowl and base *Pressed Rose*-PR01 (grey), floor shadow 'prune'.

Block 11: Wall 'lavender', floor 'raspberry', bowl and base *Pressed Rose*-PR04 (plum), floor shadow 'pomegranate'.

Block 12: Wall 'ginger', floor 'prune', bowl and base *Pressed Rose*-PR06 (coral red), floor shadow 'navy'.

Block 13: Wall 'tobacco', floor 'raspberry', bowl and base *Pressed Rose*-PR06 (coral red), floor shadow 'cassis'.

Block 14: Wall 'ginger', floor 'prune', bowl and base *Pressed Rose*-PR05 (green), floor shadow 'navy'.

Block 15: Wall 'pomegranate', floor 'pewter', bowl and base *Forget-Me-Not Rose*-GP08-J, floor shadow 'charcoal'.

Block 16: Wall 'lavender', floor 'tobacco', bowl and base *Pressed Rose*-PR05 (green), floor shadow 'pewter'.

Block 17: Wall 'lavender', floor 'slate', bowl and base *Forget-Me-Not Rose*-GP08-J, floor shadow 'navy'.

Block 18: Wall 'chartreuse', floor 'pomegranate', bowl and base *Damask*-GP02-J, floor shadow 'cassis'.

Block 19: Wall 'persimmon', floor 'smoky', bowl and base *Pressed Rose*-PR02 (gold), floor shadow 'prune'.

Block 20: Wall 'raspberry', floor 'tobacco', bowl and base *Pressed Rose*-PR01 (grey), floor shadow 'pewter'.

MAKING BLOCKS

Make each of the 20 blocks by first joining a template-PP rectangle and a template-QQ rectangle as shown in the diagram. Use the seam allowance marked on the templates. Then press the pieced block.

SEWING ON APPLIQUÉ

Take the inside-bowl appliqué piece and baste the ¼in (6mm) hem to the wrong side along the edge that joins the inside-bowl shadow appliqué, leaving the other edges unhemmed. (Cut notches in hems as necessary on curves, and finger-press to the wrong side as you baste.) Then with the right sides facing upwards, pin the inside-bowl appliqué on top of the inside-bowl shadow, overlapping the edge where they join by ¼in (6mm) and aligning the outside raw edges. Invisibly slipstitch the pieces together along the fold. Remove the basting. Baste the ¼in (6mm) hem to the wrong side around the outside edge of the joined inside-bowl pieces, and set aside.

Take the bowl appliqué piece and baste the hem to the wrong side around the outside edge of the bowl (do not turn under the edge that joins the inside bowl). With the right sides facing upwards, pin the joined inside bowl on top of the bowl, overlapping

the edge where they join by ¼in (6mm). Slipstitch the pieces together along the fold, and set aside.

Take the bowl-base appliqué and baste the hem to the wrong side around the outside edge (do not turn under the edge that joins the bowl). With the right sides facing upwards, pin the bowl on top of the bowl base, overlapping the edge where they join by ¼in (6mm). Slipstitch the pieces together along the fold, and set aside. Prepare and join on the shadow appliqué in the same way.

Press the pieced appliqué. With right sides facing upwards, pin and baste the appliqué to the large block background. Slipstitch the appliqué in place and remove all the basting. Then cut away the background fabric behind the appliqué to within about ¼in (6mm) of the slipstitching.

Make and appliqué all the blocks in the same way.

ASSEMBLING PATCHWORK
Quilt centre

Following the assembly diagram, arrange the blocks in five rows of four blocks. Using the seam allowance marked on the templates throughout, sew the blocks together in rows, then join the rows. Press.

Border

Check that the fabric-E border strips fit the sides of the quilt and trim if necessary – the appliqué might have slightly pulled in the blocks. Then sew the short strips to the top and bottom of the quilt. Join the fabric-C corner squares to the ends of the longer strips and join these borders to the sides of the quilt.

Border appliqué

Baste the hems on the circles to the wrong side and press. Baste the fabric-C circles to the border strips, positioning them in the centre of the

Quilting for Dark Rice Bowls

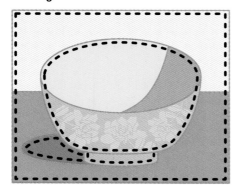

strip width and centring each one on the block it is next to, as shown in the assembly diagram. Baste one fabric-E circle to the centre of each corner square.

Slipstitch the circles in place and remove the basting.

FINISHING

Press the quilt top. Layer the quilt top, batting and backing; and baste (see page 148).

Using a greyish lavender thread, hand quilt the blocks following the diagram. On the border, hand quilt a circle ¼in (6mm) inside the outer edge of each circle.

Trim the quilt edges. Then cut the striped binding fabric on the bias and attach (see page 149).

ALTERNATIVE COLOURWAY

An alternative colourway for this patchwork was made to give you an idea of how you can make up your own colourway (see page 17).

This version is smaller than the *Dark Rice Bowls* and has a total of 12 blocks, so if you'd like to attempt making it, remember that you won't need as much fabric.

Blue-and-White Rice Bowls

The *Blue-and-White Rice Bowls* measures 42½in x 48in (108cm x 122cm) and is three blocks wide by four blocks long. The 12 blocks are

made in the same way as the blocks on the main patchwork, but they are each surrounded by 2in (5cm) wide sashing strips with 2in (5cm) squares at the intersections. An appliqué circle 1½in (4cm) in diameter (finished size) is sewn on top of each of the 20 sashing squares.

• **Wall fabrics:** At least six different solid or solid-looking small-scale monochromatic prints in pale mint green, peaches and yellows
• **Floor fabrics:** At least six different solid or solid-looking small-scale monochromatic prints in muddy pinks, lavenders and taupes
• **Floor-shadow fabric:** A single monochromatic grey-wine batik print
• **Inside-bowl fabric:** KAFFE FASSETT'S 'blush' *Shot Cotton* (SC28) or a similar solid-coloured very pale peach fabric
• **Inside-bowl-shadow fabric:** KAFFE FASSETT'S 'ecru' *Shot Cotton* (SC24) or a similar solid-coloured light taupe fabric
• **Bowl fabrics:** KAFFE FASSETT'S *Pressed Roses*-PR01 or a similar bicolour print with off-white flowers on a grey ground; *Pressed Roses*-PR03 or a similar bicolour print with white flowers on an indigo ground; and *Pressed Roses*-PR07 or a similar bicolour print with off-white flowers on a cobalt ground
• **Sashing-strip fabric:** KAFFE FASSETT'S *Blue-and-White Stripe* (BWS01) or a similar narrow, dusty blue and ecru stripe; cut 16 strips 2½in x 10in (6.5cm x 25.5cm) and 15 strips 2½in x 12in (6.5cm x 30.5cm)
• **Sashing-squares and circles fabrics:** Scraps from the wall, floor and floor-shadow fabrics; cut 20 squares 2½in x 2½in (6.5cm x 6.5cm)
• **Binding fabric:** KAFFE FASSETT'S broad *Blue-and-White Stripe* (BWS02) or a similar broad, dusty blue and ecru stripe
• **Quilting thread:** Off-white thread

pastel bubbles

The instructions that follow are for the *Pastel Bubbles* quilt (see page 19). Experienced patchworkers might like to try the quilt in an alternative colourway – fabric descriptions for another version with earthy tones are given on pages 78 and 80.

SIZE

The finished *Pastel Bubbles* measures approximately 72in x 84in (183cm x 213.5cm).

Note that measurements on the diagrams are for finished patch sizes, excluding the seam allowances.

Special note: The assortment of A and B fabrics on the quilt are used for the pinwheels, the circle appliqués, and as part of the bubble blocks and the outer border (border 4). These small-scale prints were chosen for their colours and because the themes of the prints are 'dotty' – polka dots, spots, circles or small round motifs.

INGREDIENTS

44–45in (112–114cm) wide 100% cotton fabrics:
• **Fabric A:** 1½yd (1.4m) of a print with charcoal pin dots on a white ground
• **Fabric B:** ¼yd (25cm) each of at least 13 different small-scale 'dotty' prints, all in pale-toned soft pastels that have white as one of the print colours
• **Fabric C:** ¼yd (25cm) each of at least 12 different small-scale 'dotty' prints, all in light- to medium-toned chalky pastels that have white as one of the print colours
• **Fabric D:** ¼yd (25cm) each of at least 10 different small-scale monochromatic prints, plaids and stripes, all in white-on-white or pastel-

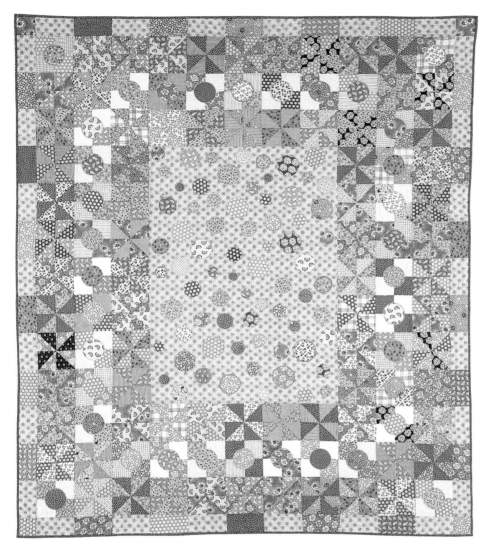

TEMPLATES

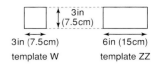

3in (7.5cm)	3in (7.5cm)	6in (15cm)
template R	template W	template ZZ

cotton fabrics using spray starch to stiffen them. Use sharp scissors to cut out the circles, and once they are cut, keep them flat and untouched to avoid frayed edges.

Drawing around the circle templates, mark and cut a total of 72 circles mostly from fabrics B and C, and a few from fabric D. Cut a random mixture of sizes – for example, the quilt centre on our patchwork has 14 circles 3½in (9cm) in diameter, four circles 3¼in (8cm) in diameter, 16 circles 2¾in (7cm) in diameter, eight circles 2½in (6.5cm) in diameter, 11 circles 2¼in (6cm in diameter), 12 circles 2in (5cm) in diameter, four circles 1¾in (4.5cm) in diameter and three circles 1⅝in (3cm) in diameter.

Borders 1–3

72 pinwheels: For each of the 72 pinwheels, cut *two sets* of four matching template-R triangles – one set from a single fabric B (pale tones) and one set from a single fabric C (medium tones).

36 bubble blocks: For each of the 36 bubble blocks, cut *two sets* of two matching template-W squares – one set from a single fabric B or C (pale or medium tones) and one set from a single fabric D ('white' tones).

36 circle appliqués: Cut a total of 36 circles 3½in (9cm) in diameter from fabrics B and C, following the tips for cutting circles for the quilt centre.

Border 4

48 rectangles: Cut 26 template-ZZ rectangles from fabric A and 22 from fabric B or C.

4 corner squares: Cut a total of four template-W squares from fabric B or C.

on-white (most of them should 'read' when viewed from a distance as practically white)

• **Backing fabric:** 5yd (4.6m)

• **Binding fabric:** ¾yd (70cm) of a print with white dots on a blue ground

• **Lightweight cotton batting:** 79in × 91in (201cm × 232cm)

• **Appliqué thread:** Assortment of threads in pastel shades for machine satin stitch around circle appliqués and fine ('lingerie') thread for the bobbin

• **Quilting thread:** Pastel pink thread

• **Templates and appliqués:** Use templates R, W and ZZ on pages 150 and 152, and make your own circle appliqué shapes as instructed

MAKING CIRCLE TEMPLATES

Using a compass and drawing on cardboard, mark *at least* six different circle appliqué sizes, ranging from the largest of 3½in (9cm) and the smallest of 1⅝in (3cm). For example, our quilt has eight circle sizes in the following diameters: 3½in, 3¼in, 2¾in, 2½in, 2¼in, 2in, 1¾in and 1⅝in (9cm, 8cm, 7cm, 6.5cm, 6cm, 5cm, 4.5cm and 3cm). Cut out the cardboard circles.

CUTTING PATCHES
Quilt centre

72 circle appliqués: For more accurate shapes, before marking and cutting the circle appliqués press the

QUILT CENTRE

For the quilt centre background, cut a large piece of fabric A measuring 44in × 32in (112cm × 81cm). With basting, mark a line 1in (2.5cm) in from the raw edge all around the border of this background piece – this is a temporary line marking the area of the quilt centre, which may alter slightly once the appliqué has been sewn on.

Press this background piece.

Sewing on appliqué

Baste the 72 circles cut for the quilt centre to the fabric-A background, placing them in random positions inside the basted line. Place sewing machine tear-away stablizer paper behind each circle, and using a thread that contrasts with the circle, secure each circle in place with machine satin stitch over the raw edge. Be sure to use a thinner sewing machine needle than normally used for piecing and a fine ('lingerie') thread in the bobbin. When all the circles have been sewn in place with satin stitch, remove the basting and tear away the stabilizer paper on the back.

Press the quilt centre, then trim it to measure 30½in × 42½in (77.5cm × 108cm).

BORDERS

Making blocks for borders 1–3

72 pinwheels: Make 72 pinwheels, joining the eight patches cut for each pinwheel (four matching pale-toned triangles and four matching medium-toned triangles) as shown in the diagram. Make sure that you position the darker triangles on each pinwheel

Pinwheel

in the same place as shown on the diagram so that all the pinwheels will appear to 'spin' in the same direction. (Use the seam allowance marked on the templates throughout.)

36 bubble blocks: Make 36 bubble blocks, joining the four patches cut for each block (two matching pale- or medium-toned squares and two matching 'white'-toned squares) as shown in the diagram. Then sew on a contrasting 3½in (9cm) circle appliqué in the same way as for the circles on the quilt centre.

Assembling border 1

For both the top and bottom borders, join five pinwheels together in a long strip, then sew to the quilt.

For each of the two side borders, join nine pinwheels and sew to the quilt.

Assembling border 2

For both the top and bottom borders, join seven bubble blocks together in a long strip, then sew to the quilt.

For each of the two side borders, join nine bubble blocks, then join a pinwheel to each end, and sew to the quilt.

Assembling border 3

For both the top and bottom borders, join nine pinwheels, then sew to the quilt.

For each of the two side borders, join 11 pinwheels, then join a bubble block to each end, and sew to the quilt.

Assembling border 4

For both the top and bottom borders, join a total of 11 template-ZZ rectangles – six fabric-A and five fabric-C or -B – alternating the fabric-A rectangles with the other rectangles. Sew to the quilt.

Bubble block

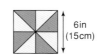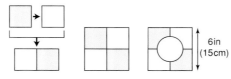

For each of the two side borders, join a total of 13 rectangles, alternating the colours as before, then join a template-W corner square to each end. Sew to the quilt.

FINISHING

Before completing the quilt you can pad each of the circle appliqués – this is optional. Slit the backing behind each circle and stuff lightly with a little batting, then sew the slit closed. If you decide not to pad the circles, cut away the background fabric behind the appliqué to within about ¼in (6mm) of the satin stitching.

Press the quilt top. Layer the quilt top, batting and backing; and baste (see page 148).

Using a pastel pink thread, machine-quilt a circle inside each circle patch right next to the inside edge of the satin stitch. Machine-quilt all over the rest of the quilt with swirls and circles, incorporating circles that swirl around outside the circle patches.

Trim the quilt edges. Then cut the binding fabric and attach (see page 149 for how to do this).

ALTERNATIVE COLOURWAY

An alternative colourway (see page 21) was made to show how different the patchwork looks in another scheme, and to give you an idea of how you can make up your own colourway.

Byzantine Bubbles

The *Byzantine Bubbles* quilt was made in the same way as the main quilt, but with different colours and with the pinwheel blocks 'spinning' in both directions (see instructions for pinwheel blocks for explanation). Follow the colour descriptions given below; and if desired, use KAFFE FASSETT'S 'circus' and 'blue and white' *Roman Glass* (GP01-C and GP01-BW)

ASSEMBLY

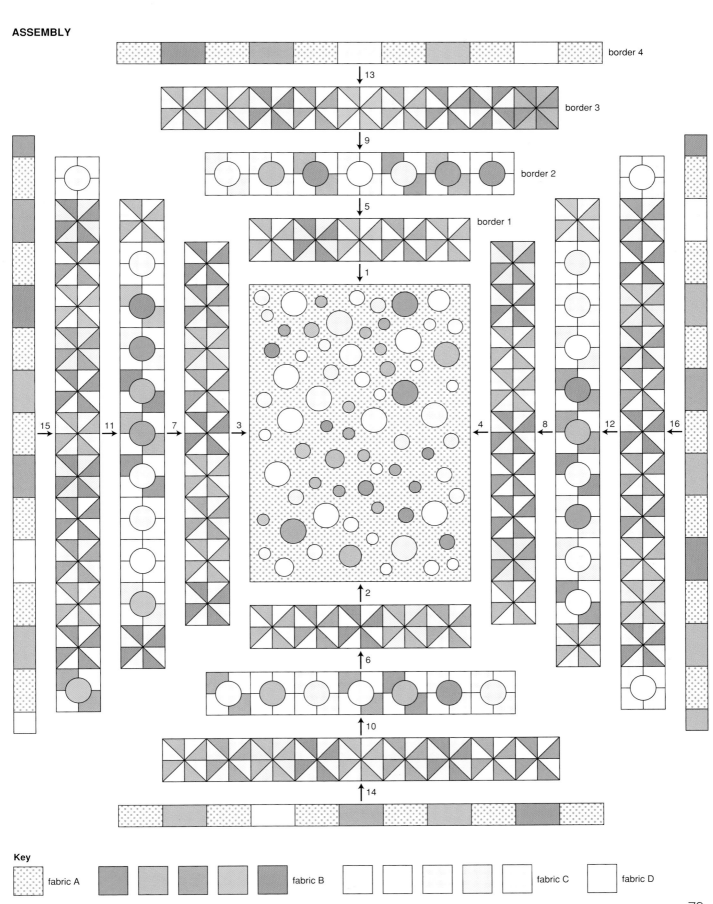

border 4

border 3

border 2

border 1

Key

fabric A

fabric B

fabric C

fabric D

for some of the appliqué circles and on some pinwheel blocks, as we did.

- **Fabric A:** KAFFE FASSETT's 'gold' *Roman Glass* (GP01-G) or a similar medium-scale circles print with a gold ground and jewel-coloured accents
- **Fabric B:** Dark-toned, small-scale 'dotty' prints, predominantly in ochres, and autumn-leaf and earth shades, plus accents of dusty lavenders, muddy teals and wine-stain reds
- **Fabric C:** Medium-toned, small-scale 'dotty' prints in same colours as fabric B
- **Fabric D:** Medium- and medium-light-toned monochromatic prints in caramel golds
- **Binding fabric:** KAFFE FASSETT's *Broad Stripe* (BS11) or a similar multi-coloured, mainly gold and rust, broad stripe (cut strips on the bias for binding)
- **Appliqué thread:** Bright yellow thread
- **Quilting thread:** Gold-coloured thread

suzani quilt

Many KAFFE FASSETT fabrics were used in the *Suzani Quilt*, because they tied in nicely with the colour theme. Incorporate these fabrics in your version of the patchwork if you like (see page 159 for fabric information), or chose ones in similar shades.

SIZE
The finished patchwork measures approximately 70in x 70in (175cm x 175cm).
Note that measurements on the diagrams are for finished patch sizes, excluding the seam allowances.

INGREDIENTS
44–45in (112–114cm) wide 100% cotton fabrics:
- **Fabric A:** ¼–½yd (25–46cm) each of

at least 10 different monochromatic small- and medium-scale spot, dot and circles prints in medium to medium-light tones of golden ochres and rusty oranges
- **Fabric B:** ¾yd (70cm) of KAFFE FASSETT's 'mustard' *Shot Cotton* (SC16) and ¼yd (25cm) each of 'tangerine', 'chartreuse' (deep chartreuse) and 'tobacco' (tobacco brown) *Shot Cotton* (SC11, SC12 and SC18), or four similar solid-coloured fabrics
- **Fabric C:** ¾yd (70cm) of KAFFE FASSETT's 'raspberry' (raspberry red) *Shot Cotton* (SC08), ½yd (46cm) of 'pomegranate' (pomegranate red) *Shot Cotton* (SC09), and ¼yd (25cm) of 'cassis' (deep wine red) *Shot Cotton* (SC02), or three similar solid-coloured fabrics
- **Fabric D:** ¼yd (25cm) each of KAFFE FASSETT's 'opal' (lavender-blue) and 'smoky' (grey-blue) *Shot Cotton* (SC05 and SC20), or two similar solid-coloured fabrics
- **Fabric E (outer border):** 1yd (91cm) of KAFFE FASSETT's 'gold' *Roman Glass* (GP01-G) or a similar medium-scale circles print with a gold ground and jewel-coloured accents
- **Fabric F:** ½yd (46cm) of KAFFE FASSETT's 'ginger' *Shot Cotton* (SC01) and ¾yd (70cm) each of 'persimmon' (orange-red) and 'bittersweet' (dusty orange) *Shot Cotton* (SC07 and SC10), or three similar solid-coloured fabrics
- **Binding fabric for circles:** 1yd (91cm) of KAFFE FASSETT's *Broad Stripe*-BS01 or a similar broad, multi-coloured stripe mainly in reds
- **Backing fabric:** 4½yd (4.2m)
- **Binding fabric for quilt:** ¾yd (70cm) of KAFFE FASSETT's *Broad Stripe*-BS11 or a similar broad, multi-coloured stripe mainly in gold and rust
- **Lightweight cotton batting:** 77in x 77in (193cm x 193cm)
- **Quilting thread:** Twisted cotton

embroidery thread in golds, reds and deep pink

CUTTING PATCHES
Quilt centre
36 large squares: Cut 36 squares 8½in x 8½in (21.5cm x 21.5cm) from fabric A.

13 circle appliqués: The circles are cut from solid-coloured fabrics that form part of the fabric B, C and F groups. For more accurate shapes, before marking and cutting the appliqué circles press the cotton fabrics using spray starch to stiffen them. Cut four circles 18in (45.5cm) in diameter – one from 'mustard', one from 'raspberry', one from 'persimmon' and one from 'bittersweet' (dusty orange). Cut one circle 10½in (26.5cm) in diameter from 'ginger'. Cut four circles 5½in (14cm) in diameter – two from 'raspberry' and two from 'pomegranate'. Cut four circles 4in (10cm) in diameter – one from 'pomegranate', one from 'persimmon' and two from 'bittersweet' (dusty orange).

Circles binding: From striped binding fabric for circles, cut 2in (5cm) wide strips on the bias and join into a continuous strip at least 12yd (11m) long.

Inner border
112 snowball squares: Cut 112 squares 4½in x 4½in (11.5cm x 11.5cm) from fabrics A and B.

224 red corner tabs: Cut 224 squares 1½in x 1½in (4cm x 4cm) from fabric C.

Snowball block

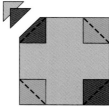
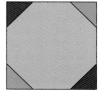

1. Stitch and trim   2. Press open

ASSEMBLY

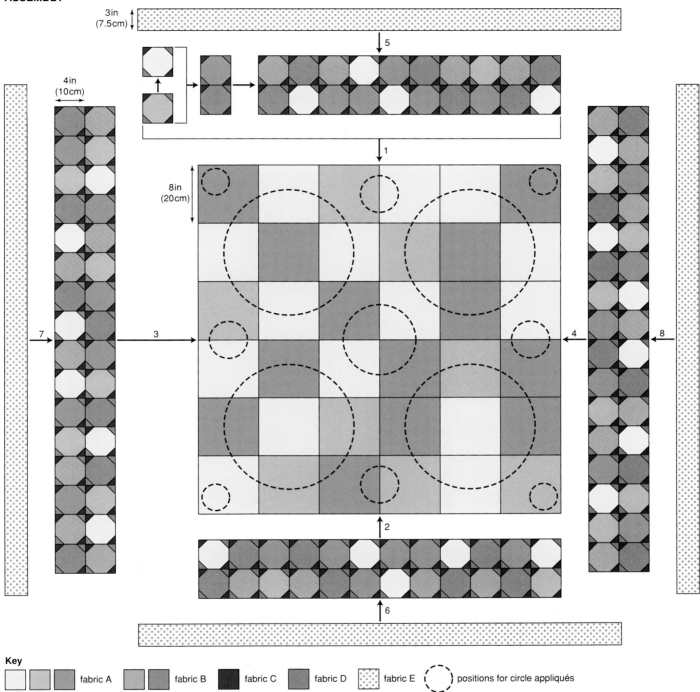

3in
(7.5cm)

4in
(10cm)

8in
(20cm)

5

1

7   3   4   8

2

6

Key

fabric A   fabric B   fabric C   fabric D   fabric E   ( ) positions for circle appliqués

224 blue corner tabs: Cut 224 squares 1½in × 1½in (4cm × 4cm) from fabric D.

Outer border

4 strips: From fabric E, cut two strips 3½in × 64½in (9cm × 161.5cm) and two strips 3½in × 70½in (9cm × 176.5cm), piecing as required.

MAKING SNOWBALL BLOCKS

To form the corner tabs on each snowball block, select two different 1½in (4cm) fabric-C (red) squares and two different fabric-D (blue) squares. Fold the small squares in half diagonally, finger-press to crease the diagonal fold, then unfold. Place a red square on one

corner of the 4½in (11.5cm) snowball square with the right sides facing and the edges aligned. Stitch along the diagonal crease. Stitch a red square to the diagonally opposite corner in the same way, then a blue square to each of the two remaining corners. Trim off the outside triangles ¼in (6mm)

in quietly with the stripe. Bind all the circles in the same way. If you have used stabilizer paper, tear it away. Cut away the background fabric behind the circles to within ¼in (6mm) of the binding seam.

ASSEMBLING INNER BORDER
Arrange two rows of snowball blocks all around the quilt centre, either on the floor or on a cotton-flannel design wall. Position the blocks so that the red corner tabs are always in the upper left-hand and lower right-hand corners. Once you have achieved the desired effect, sew together the blocks at the top of the quilt centre as shown in the assembly diagram, making a border two blocks deep and 12 blocks long and using a ¼in (7.5mm) seam allowance throughout. Sew to the top of the quilt centre.
Join the blocks for the bottom border in the same way and sew to the quilt. Then join the blocks for the two sides and sew them to the quilt.

ASSEMBLING OUTER BORDER
Sew the short fabric-E strips to the top and bottom of the quilt, and then sew the long fabric-E strips to the sides.

FINISHING
Press the quilt top. Layer the quilt top, batting and backing; and baste (see page 148).
Using embroidery thread in a contrasting colour thread, hand quilt irregular wavy parallel lines across the circle appliqués and then the quilt centre background. Hand quilt two concentric circles inside each snowball block, then a large rounded, irregular zigzag along each outer border strip. Trim the quilt edges. Then cut the striped binding fabric on the bias and attach (see page 149).

beyond this new seam as shown in the diagram. Then press the corner tab triangles away from the centre of the snowball block.
Sew two red and two blue corner tabs to each of the remaining snowball squares in the same way.

ASSEMBLING QUILT CENTRE
Arrange the 8½in (21.5cm) squares in six rows of six squares positioning the colours at random. Do this on the floor or on a cotton-flannel design wall (see page 144). Once you have achieved the desired effect, sew the patches together in rows, then join the rows, using a ¼in (7.5mm) seam allowance throughout. Press the quilt centre.

CIRCLES APPLIQUÉ
Following the assembly diagram for the positions, arrange the circles on the quilt centre. Pin and baste the circles in place, then remove the pins. Next, stitch the striped circles binding around each circle. To do this, first fold the continuous binding in half lengthways and press. Keeping the binding folded in half and being careful not to stretch it, baste it around the circle aligning the raw edges with the raw edge of the circle. Where the ends of the binding meet, fold in the end at one end and tuck the other end inside it as you do when binding your quilt (see page 149). Machine-stitch the binding in place ¼in (6mm) from the raw edges (use a sewing machine tear-away stabilizer paper behind the background fabric if desired). Remove the basting. Press the bias binding away from the centre of the circle and topstitch close to the folded edge of the binding with a colour that blends

hat boxes quilt

The hat boxes and the 'wallpapers' in the cubbyholes on this quilt are made from an assortment of scraps. If you are using furnishing/decorating fabrics for many of the hat boxes as we did, try to use regular quilting fabric for the backgrounds to keep the overall weight of the quilt under control.

SIZE

The finished patchwork measures approximately 91½in × 91½in (232.5cm × 232.5cm).
Note that measurements on the diagrams are for finished patch sizes, excluding the seam allowances.

INGREDIENTS

100% cotton quilt fabrics and furnishing/decorating fabrics:
• **Fabric A (wallpapers):** Assortment of scraps of small- to medium-scale mostly monochromatic florals in blue-greens, grey-lavenders, grey-blues, dark reds, dusty pinks and ochres – collect light to medium tones in these shades for side 'walls' and co-ordinating medium to dark tones for 'backgrounds' (square patches)
• **Fabric B (floor stripes):** ½yd (46cm) each of KAFFE FASSETT'S *Ombré Stripes* (OS01, OS02, OS04 and OS05) in green, blue, brown and pink/purple (all on ecru grounds), or four similar ombré stripes
• **Fabric C (hat boxes):** Assortment of scraps of 'toile' prints and similar large-scale florals in grey-greens, wine reds, blues, golds and a brown, all on ecru or matching palely tinged grounds; plus an assortment of large-scale muted florals, predominantly with flowers in rose pinks, grey-green leaves and ecru grounds
• **Fabric D (hat box rims):** Assortment of stripes, checks, medium- and small-

scale prints in same colours as boxes
• **Fabric E (sashing squares):** ¼yd (25cm) of a blue-green mini-print with gold accents
• **Fabric F (sashing strips):** 1½yd (1.4m) of a beige mini-print
• **Fabric G (borders):** Total of at least 1½yd (1.4m) of three large-scale two-tone 'toile' prints in blue, aqua and grey-green, all on ecru grounds
• **Backing fabric:** 8yd (7.3m)
• **Binding fabric:** 1yd (91cm) of an 'old-fashioned' lavender plaid
• **Lightweight cotton batting:** 99in × 99in (250cm × 250cm)

TEMPLATES

• **Appliqué thread:** Very bright scarlet red thread
• **Quilting thread:** Deep ecru thread
• **Templates and appliqués:** Use templates J, J reverse, K, L and M, and appliqué shapes on page 155, enlarging them as instructed

CUTTING PATCHES
Quilt centre

Note: If you have a fabric scrap for a wallpaper patch or a hat box patch that is too small, piece together similar fabrics to make a large remnant, and then cut the patch from that.

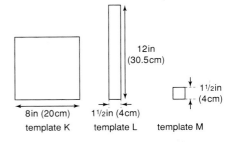

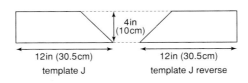

12in (30.5cm)
template J

12in (30.5cm)
template J reverse

4in (10cm)

8in (20cm)
template K

1½in (4cm)
template L

12in (30.5cm)

1½in (4cm)
template M

Window block

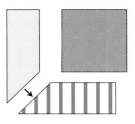 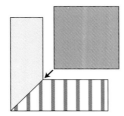 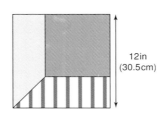

12in
(30.5cm)

36 paired wallpapers: For each of the 36 cubbyholes, cut a template-J trapezoid from a light- to medium-toned fabric A and a template-K square from a slightly darker, similarly coloured fabric A.

36 floor stripes: For the cubbyhole floors, cut 36 template-J-reverse trapezoids from fabric B, with the stripes running parallel to the short, straight side of the template.

36 hat boxes: For each of the 36 hat boxes, cut a hat-box bottom and a hat-box top mostly from the same fabric C, but mismatching the top and bottom patches on some of the hat boxes. Then cut a hat box rim patch from fabric D in a shade that contrasts with both the hat box top and bottom.

49 sashing squares: Cut 49 template-M sashing squares from fabric E.

84 sashing strips: Cut 84 template-L sashing strips from fabric F.

Border

Border strips: Cut the border fabrics (fabric G) into 6½in (16.5cm) wide strips, then cut these strips into random lengths between 5½in (14cm) and 17½in (44.5cm) long.

MAKING BLOCKS

36 blocks: Make 36 window blocks, joining a template-J and a template-J-reverse trapezoid for each block along the diagonal as shown in the diagram, then stitching on a template-K square with an inset seam. (Use the seam allowance marked on the templates throughout.)

HAT BOX APPLIQUÉ

Press the blocks flat, then join the appliqué to each block. First, baste the hat box bottom to the block. Using the bright scarlet red thread, machine stitch with buttonhole or blanket stitch from A to B as shown on the diagram (use sewing machine tear-away stablizer paper behind the background fabric if desired). Next, baste on the hat box top, and stitch from C to D in scarlet red thread as before. Remove the basting threads, then baste the contrasting hat box rim in place, overlapping the top and bottom of the box. Stitch from E to F in scarlet red thread as before. Remove the basting, and if you have used stabilizer paper on the back, tear it away. Press.

Quilting for Hat Boxes Quilt

Cut away the background fabric behind the box to within about ¼in (6mm) of the scarlet edging stitches.

MAKING BORDER

Stitch the border strips together into one continuous 6½in (16.5cm) wide strip at least 9yd 26in (8.9m) long, alternating the fabrics. Then cut into two 80in (204cm) lengths and two 92in (234cm) lengths for the four border strips.

ASSEMBLING PATCHWORK
Quilt centre

Following the assembly diagram, arrange the hat boxes in six rows of six blocks, and place the sashing strips and squares around them. Make the arrangement on the floor or on a cotton-flannel design wall (see page 144). Once you have achieved the desired effect, sew the patches together in rows, then join the rows.

Border

Join the two shorter pieced strips to the sides of the quilt centre, then join the longer strips to the top and bottom.

FINISHING

Press the quilt top. Layer the quilt top, batting and backing; and baste (see page 148).

Using a deep ecru thread, machine-

Hat box appliqué

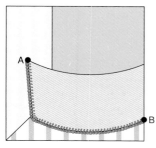 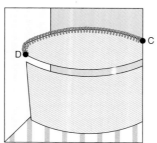 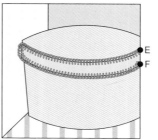

A
B
D
C
E
F

ASSEMBLY

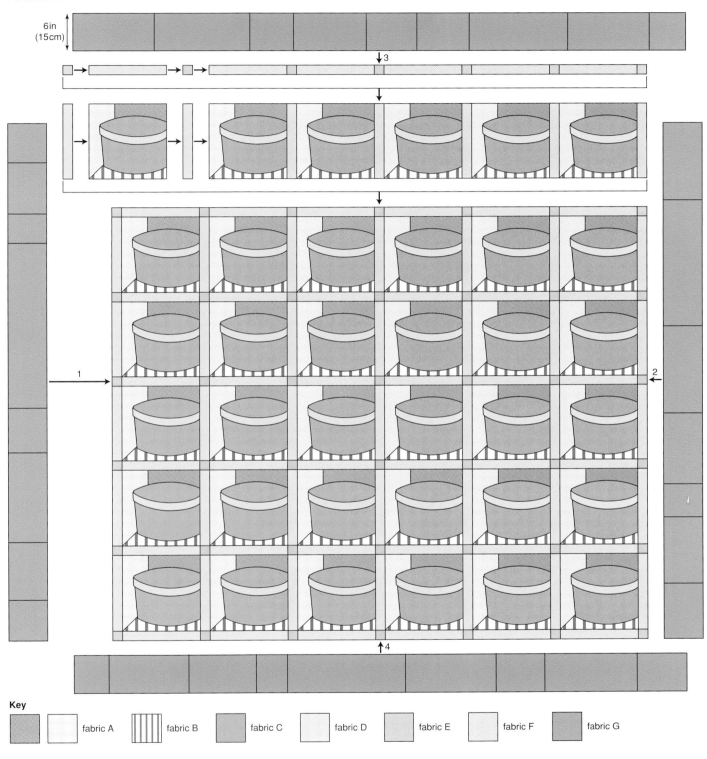

6in
(15cm)

Key

fabric A   fabric B   fabric C   fabric D   fabric E   fabric F   fabric G

quilt a pair of wavy parallel lines along the sashing strips and a spiral in each sashing square as shown in quilting diagram. Then machine-quilt squiggles on the 'wallpaper' to imitate the fabric print, parallel lines on the striped floors to emphasize the stripes, and outline quilt the hat boxes to echo the shapes as shown in the diagram. Lastly, machine-quilt squiggles on the outside border, roughly following the designs on the 'toile' prints.

Trim the quilt edges. Then cut the binding fabric and attach (see page 149 for how to do this).

gypsy garden

Gypsy Garden has three alternative colourways. Each version is built around one of the colourways of a KAFFE FASSETT fabric called *Flower Lattice*, which is a very large-scale diaper-pattern floral with a strong diagonal grid of tight leaves. The large squares in the quilt centre are all cut from this fabric, and the *Flower Lattice* colourway determines the mood and coloration of the checkerboards that are paired with it. The instructions are written for the *Gypsy Garden* (see page 27), and the fabric descriptions for other versions are given on pages 88 and 89.

SIZE

The finished *Gypsy Garden* patchwork measures approximately 87½in × 104¾in (216cm × 259.5cm).

Note that any measurements on the diagrams are for finished patch sizes, excluding the seam allowances.

INGREDIENTS

44–45in (112–114cm) wide 100% cotton fabrics:

Quilt Centre

• **Fabric A:** 2½yd (2.3m) of KAFFE FASSETT's 'jewel' *Flower Lattice* (GP11-J) or a similar large-scale floral with green leaves and dark pink flowers on a black ground

• **Fabric B:** ¼yd (25cm) each of at least 15 different medium-scale florals or leaf prints that have deep reds and greens as the predominant colours

• **Fabric C:** ¼yd (25cm) each of at least 15 different fabrics in a mixture of solids and solid-looking small-scale prints, dots and plaids, predominantly in dark plums, navy, ochres and maroons

Border fabrics

• **Fabric D:** 1½yd (1.4m) of KAFFE FASSETT's 'pomegranate' *Shot Cotton*

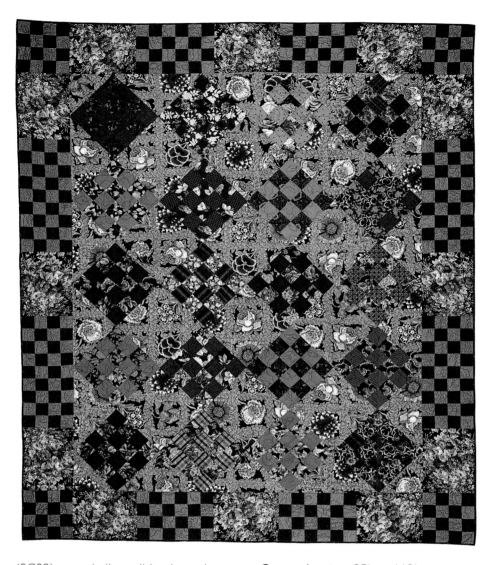

(SC09) or a similar solid-coloured pomegranate red fabric

• **Fabric E:** 2yd (1.8m) of a monochromatic bright moss green print (almost solid looking)

• **Fabric F:** ½yd (46cm) of KAFFE FASSETT's 'charcoal' *Shot Cotton* (SC25) or a similar solid-coloured charcoal fabric

• **Fabric G:** 2yd (1.8m) of a medium-scale voluptuous floral bouquet print with dark pink flowers and green leaves on a black ground

• **Backing fabric:** 8yd (7.3m)

• **Binding fabric:** 1yd (91cm) of KAFFE FASSETT's *Narrow Stripe*-NS09 or a similar narrow, dark plummy multi-coloured stripe for a bias binding

• **Cotton batting:** 95in × 112in (234cm × 278cm)

• **Quilting thread:** Red thread

CUTTING PATCHES

Quilt centre

12 large squares: From fabric A, cut 12 squares 12½in × 12½in (31.5cm × 31.5cm). DO NOT fussy cut fabric A (i.e., do not centre the flowers).

14 edging triangles: From fabric A, cut seven squares 12⅞in × 12⅞in (32.5cm × 32.5cm), then cut each one in half diagonally from corner to corner to form 14 triangles (see Cutting note).

4 corner triangles: From fabric A, cut one square 13⅜in × 13⅜in (34cm × 34cm), then cut it from corner to corner both ways to form four triangles (see Cutting note).

Cutting note: The cutting of the edge and corner triangles as described above, puts the bias edge of the fabric on the outside (see Fabric Grain Line diagrams). The tight leaf-pattern in the jewel *Flower Lattice* makes a strong grid appearance in the blocks, and cutting in this direction continues the pattern to the edge of the quilt centre. The outside border remedies the problem of having a bias on the edge. On the other versions of this quilt, which have no outside border, the edge triangles are cut so that the outside edge follows the fabric grain. If you chose to do this pattern without

ASSEMBLY

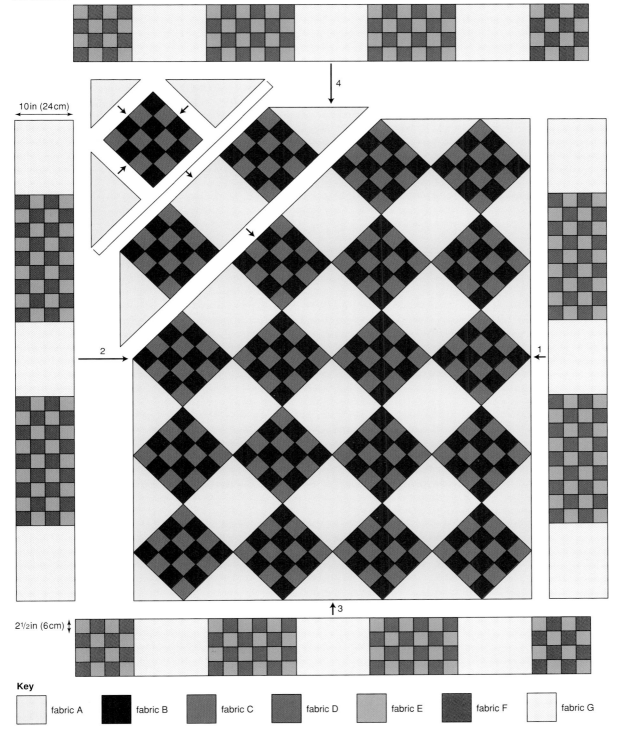

10in (24cm)

2¹/₂in (6cm)

Key

| | fabric A | | fabric B | | fabric C | | fabric D | | fabric E | | fabric F | | fabric G |

Fabric grain lines for Gypsy Garden

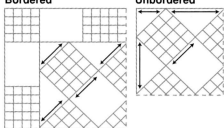

an outside border, cut the 12⅞in × 12⅞in (32.5cm × 32.5cm) squares as if they were diamonds with the bias edges on the outside of the squares, then bisect; the straight grain will end up on the long side where you want it.

20 large checkerboard blocks: For each of the 20 large checkerboard blocks, cut *two sets* of eight squares 3½in × 3½in (9cm × 9cm), using a single B fabric for one set and a single C fabric for the other set. (A total of 16 squares for each block.)

Border
304 checkerboard squares: Cut 120 squares 3in × 3in (7.5cm × 7.5cm) from fabric D (pomegranate red), 152 from fabric E (moss green) and 32 from fabric F (charcoal).

12 floral rectangles: From fabric G (floral), cut six rectangles 13¾in × 10½in (36cm × 25.5cm) and six rectangles 13in × 10½in (34cm × 25.5cm).

QUILT CENTRE
Making blocks
20 large checkerboard blocks: Using a ¼in (7.5mm) seam allowance throughout, make 20 large checkerboard blocks, joining the 16 squares cut for each block as shown in the diagram,

Large checkerboard block

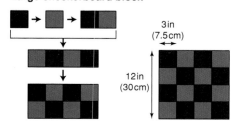

so that the fabric-B and fabric-C patches alternate.

Assembling quilt centre
Following the assembly diagram, arrange the blocks, large squares and triangles on the floor or on a cotton-flannel design wall (see page 144). Once you have achieved the desired effect, sew the blocks and patches together in diagonal rows, then join the rows.

BORDER
Making checkerboard rectangles
4 four-by-nine checkerboards: Make four checkerboard rectangles four rows by nine rows, each with 18 fabric-D squares (pomegranate red) and 18 fabric-E squares (moss green), first sewing the patches together into four rows of nine, then joining the rows.

4 four-by-six checkerboards: Make four checkerboard rectangles four rows by six rows, each with 12 fabric-D squares (pomegranate red) and 12 fabric-E squares (moss green), first sewing the patches together into four rows of six, then joining the four rows.

4 four-by-four corner checkerboards: Make four corner checkerboards four rows by four rows, each with 8 fabric-F squares (charcoal) and 8 fabric-E squares (moss green), first sewing the patches together into four rows of four, then joining the four rows.

Assembling border
For each of the two side borders, join three of the larger fabric-G (floral) rectangles to two of the four-by-nine checkerboards as shown in the assembly diagram. Since there are bias-cut edges on the quilt centre, pin the side borders to the centre and baste if necessary. Then machine stitch, placing the quilt centre down against the sewing machine feed dogs to help ease in. For both the top and bottom borders, join three of the smaller fabric-G (floral) rectangles to two of the four-

by-six checkerboards, then sew a four-by-four corner checkerboard to each end. Sew the top and bottom borders to the quilt as for the side borders.

FINISHING
Press the quilt top. Layer the quilt top, batting and backing; and baste (see page 148).

Using red thread, machine-quilt the entire patchwork with a large, simple floral motif. Trim the quilt edges. Then cut the striped binding fabric on the bias and attach (see page 149).

ALTERNATIVE COLOURWAYS
The alternative versions of this quilt are made without the wide borders (see pages 29, 30 and 31). You can make them with a four-by-five checkerboard block arrangement (as the *Gypsy Garden*) for a finished size of approximately 67½in × 84¾in (169.5cm × 211.5cm), or a five-by-five arrangement for a finished size of approximately 84¾in × 84¾in (211.5cm × 211.5cm). But if making a five-by-five arrangement, cut 16 (instead of 12) large fabric-A squares, make 25 (instead of 20) large checkerboard blocks, and cut 16 (instead of 14) edging triangles.

If you are an experienced patchworker and would like to try one of these alternatives, follow the main instructions, but omit the borders.

Ghost Garden
• **Fabric A:** KAFFE FASSETT's 'stone' *Flower Lattice* (GP11-S) or a similar large-scale floral with pale buttermilk flowers and grey leaves on a dark grey ground
• **Fabric B:** Medium-scale florals and leaf prints, predominantly in dusty shades of peaches, pinks and a couple of golds and greens
• **Fabric C:** Plaids, stripes, small-scale prints and solids, predominantly in greys, sand, muddy to grey tones of

lavender, cinammon, and greeny taupe
- **Binding fabric:** KAFFE FASSETT's grey *Pressed Roses* (PR01) or a similar bicolour print with off-white flowers on a grey ground

Honey Garden

Unlike the other alternatives, *Honey Garden* has a 1½in (4cm) wide border (see page 31).
- **Fabric A:** KAFFE FASSETT's 'pastel' *Flower Lattice* (GP11-P) or a similar large-scale floral with warm ochre leaves and pale green, lilac and burgundy flowers on a grey ground
- **Fabric B:** Medium-scale florals and leaf prints, predominantly in dusty pinks, pale green, buttermilk, cinnamon and lavender
- **Fabric C:** Plaids, stripes, small-scale prints and solids, predominantly in greys, yellows, dusty wines and apple greens
- **Border fabric:** KAFFE FASSETT's pink/purple *Ombré Stripe* (OS05) or a similar pink/purple and ecru ombré stripe
- **Binding fabric:** Apple green and lilac plaid

Spring Garden

This version was made entirely with KAFFE FASSETT quilt fabrics, but you can choose your own fabrics to make it. Fabrics B and C were selected from a mixture of KAFFE FASSETT prints in colours that suit the overall scheme.
- **Fabric A:** 'Leafy' *Flower Lattice* (GP11-L) or a similar large-scale floral with sage green leaves and scarlet, maroon and pale pink flowers on a deep taupe ground
- **Fabric B:** Medium-scale floral, leaf and circular prints, predominantly in lavenders, scarlets, terracotta and golds
- **Fabric C:** Medium-scale floral, leaf and circular prints, predominantly in greys and greens and one solid blue-green ('grass' *Shot Cotton*-SC27)
- **Binding fabric:** 'Leafy' *Roman Glass* (GP01-L) or a similar medium-scale green circles print

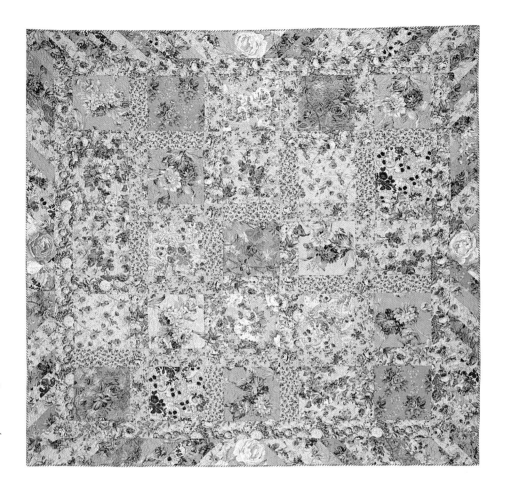

japanese brocades

The fabrics in this quilt all have a muted, soft antique look, and the overall effect is of a dipped-in-tea concoction (see pages 32 and 33). The Kaffe Fassett Designers Guild furnishing fabric 'lilac' *Rosamundi* makes an appearance in the centre of the outer border (fabric E).

SIZE

The finished patchwork measures approximately 96in x 96in (240cm x 240cm).
Note that measurements on the diagrams are for finished patch sizes, excluding the seam allowances.

Special note: Some of the patches for this quilt are 'fussy cut'. This means paying attention to the position of the flowers when cutting, and framing them carefully within the patch shape. When 'fussy cutting', it is still important to cut the patches so that they run with the grain of the fabric and not on the bias.

INGREDIENTS

44–45in (112–114cm) wide 100% cotton quilt fabrics, and light- to medium-weight furnishing/decorating fabrics (many with a brocade texture), all in floral prints with flowers in predominantly peach, rose and pinks on grounds in varying colours:
- **Fabric A:** ½yd (46cm) each of at least 15–18 different extra-large-scale florals with grounds in dusty pinks, sages, taupe and putty
- **Fabric B:** 1yd (91cm) of a medium-scale rose print with a sage ground
- **Fabric C:** At least ½yd (46cm) each

ASSEMBLY

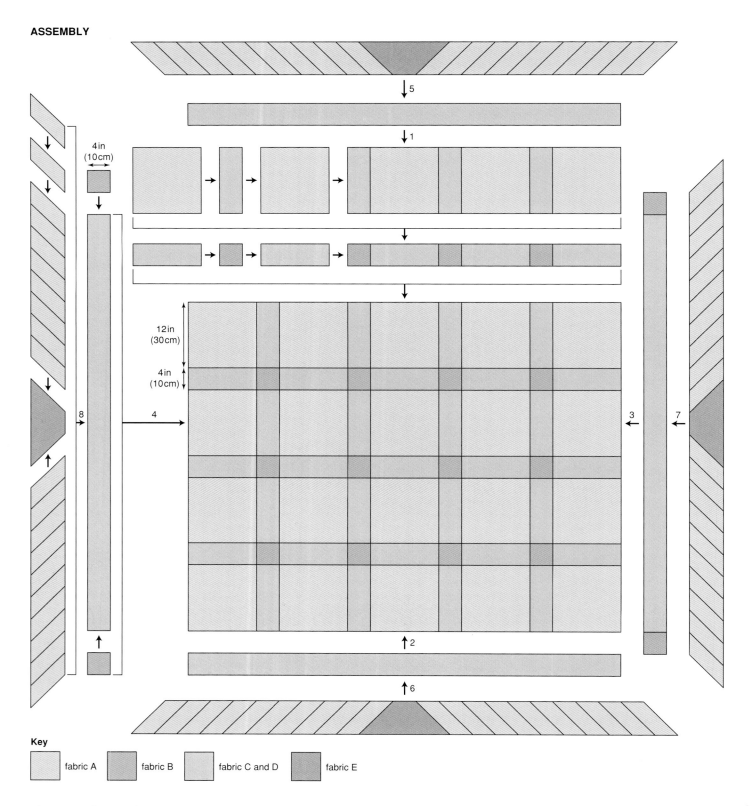

Key

fabric A   fabric B   fabric C and D   fabric E

of two small-scale florals with a dusty aqua ground
• **Fabric D:** 1½yd (1.5m) of a large-scale floral with an eau-de-nil ground
• **Fabric E:** ½yd (46cm) of an extra-

large-scale rose print
• **Backing fabric:** 8yd (7.3m)
• **Binding fabric:** 1yd (91cm) of a dusty rose and ecru stripe
• **Cotton batting:** 103in × 103in

(258cm × 258cm)
• **Quilting thread:** Pink thread
• **Templates:** Use templates Y, Y reverse and Z on pages 156 and 157

TEMPLATES

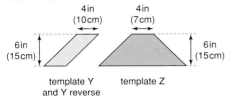

template Y
and Y reverse   template Z

CUTTING PATCHES

Inner border

Cut the inner-border patches before cutting the quilt-centre patches, so that whatever is left over of fabric D can be used for the quilt centre.

4 long strips: From fabric D, cut four strips 4½in x 76½in (11.5cm x 191.5cm) – you will need to piece this fabric to get the required length.

4 small corner squares: From fabric B, fussy cut four small squares 4½in x 4½in (11.5cm x 11.5cm).

Quilt centre

Cut the quilt-centre patches before cutting the outer-border patches, so that whatever is left over of fabric A can be used for the outer borders.

25 large squares: From fabric A, fussy cut 25 large squares 12½in x 12½in (31.5cm x 31.5cm).

16 small sashing squares: From fabric B, fussy cut 16 small squares 4½in x 4½in (11.5cm x 11.5cm).

40 sashing strips: From fabric C and remaining fabric D, cut a total of 40 strips 4½in x 12½in (11.5cm x 31.5cm).

Outer border

80 parallelograms: From remaining scraps of fabric A, cut 40 template-Y patches and 40 Y-reverse patches.

4 trapezoids: From fabric E, fussy cut four template-Z patches.

ASSEMBLING PATCHWORK

Quilt centre

Following the assembly diagram, arrange the large square patches in five rows of five, and place the sashing strips and fabric-B squares in between these large squares. Make the

arrangement on the floor or on a cotton-flannel design wall (see page 144). Once you have achieved the desired effect, sew the patches together in rows, then join the rows, using a ¼in (7.5mm) seam allowance throughout.

Inner border

Sew a long fabric-D strip to the top and the bottom of the quilt centre. Sew a fabric-B corner square to each end of the two remaining fabric-D strips, then join the strips to the sides of the quilt centre.

Outer border

For each of the four outer border strips, sew ten template-Y patches together and ten Y-reverse patches, then join these to a template-Z patch (using the seam allowance marked on the templates). Pin the borders to the quilt, carefully matching the corner

points of the seam lines. Backstitching at each end, machine stitch the borders in place starting and stopping at the corner points of the seam line to leave the mitre seam allowances free. Join each mitred corner by stitching from the outside edge of the outer border to the inner corner and backstitching at the end.

FINISHING

Press the quilt top. Layer the quilt top, batting and backing; and baste (see page 148).

Using pink thread, machine-quilt the entire patchwork in a dense continuous meandering stitch, making swirls and simple flower and leaf shapes.

Trim the quilt edges. Then cut the pink-and-ecru stripe binding fabric on the bias and attach (see page 149).

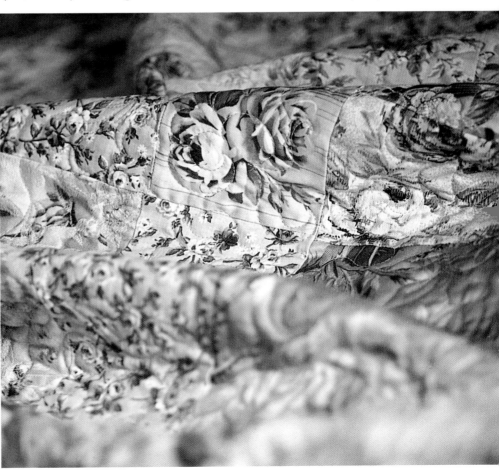

moody blues

The overall effect of the *Moody Blues* quilt is a smear of blue with zingy magenta and gold accents pinging out (see also, page 35). There are fabric descriptions for an alternative colourway, *Moody Whites*, on page 95 – you might like to try this version if you are an experienced patchworker.

The *Moody Whites* quilt has a simple strip border rather than an 'on point' border, so it is easier to change its size.

SIZE
The finished *Moody Blues* measures approximately 88in x 88in (224cm x 224cm). *Note that any measurements on the diagrams are for finished patch sizes, excluding the seam allowances.*

Special note: The dimensions of *Moody Blues* cannot be easily altered, because the inner border is 'on point' and the quilt centre is not. The border and the quilt centre fit together in very few combinations. If you do wish to make a different size, you may consider adding simple border strips around the quilt centre instead as on the *Moody Whites* version.

INGREDIENTS

44–45in (112–114cm) wide 100% cotton fabrics – the assorted scrap fabrics are in mostly monochromatic prints, simple stripes and plaids, and some dots:

- **Fabric A:** Scraps of an assortment of medium-light blue-greens (adding up to a total of approximately 1yd/1m)
- **Fabric B:** Scraps of an assortment of medium-light chalky blues and a few lavenders (adding up to approximately 1yd/1m)
- **Fabric C:** Scraps of an assortment of medium-dark moss and teal greens (adding up to a total of approximately 1yd/1m)
- **Fabric D:** Scraps of an assortment of medium-dark blues (adding up to a total of approximately 1yd/1m)
- **Fabric X:** Scraps of an assortment of very bright magentas, golds and hot pinks
- **Fabric E:** Scraps of an assortment of medium-toned muddy greens, olives and ochres (adding up to a total of approximately ¾yd/70cm)
- **Fabric F:** Scraps of an assortment of medium dull blues, plums and greyish lavender (adding up to approximately ¾yd/70cm)
- **Fabric G:** ½yd (46cm) of a single solid cobalt blue
- **Fabric H:** ½yd (46cm) of a small-scale magenta and green floral print on a navy ground
- **Fabric I:** ¾yd (70cm) of a dark maroon, blue and green woven stripe
- **Fabric J:** ¼yd (25cm) of an ochre and cobalt blue check
- **Fabric K:** 1yd (91cm) of a multi-coloured stripe (see binding)
- **Backing fabric:** 8yd (7.3m)
- **Binding fabric:** 1yd (91cm) extra of fabric K for bias binding
- **Cotton batting:** 95in x 95in (242cm x 242cm)
- **Quilting thread:** Deep green or deep blue thread
- **Templates:** Use templates R, S, T, U and V on pages 150, 151, 152 and 153

CUTTING PATCHES
Quilt centre

From fabric A: Cut 98 matching pairs of template-R squares, for a total of 196 squares.

From fabric B: As for fabric A.

From fabric C: As for fabric A.

From fabric D: As for fabric A.

From fabric X: Cut 392 squares 1½in x 1½in (4cm x 4cm).

Inner border

From fabric E: Cut 44 matching pairs of template-R squares, for a total of 88 squares.

From fabric F: As for fabric E.

From fabric G: Cut 40 template-R squares.

From fabric H: Cut 80 template-S triangles.

From fabric I: Cut 40 template-T triangles, paying attention to the direction of the stripes.

From fabric J: Cut four template-U corner triangles.

Outer border

From fabric X: Cut 80 template-V triangles.

From fabric K: Cut 20 strips 2½in x 15¾in (6.5cm x 40cm).

QUILT CENTRE
Making blocks

98 A-B four-patch blocks: Make 98 A-B four-patch blocks, joining two matching fabric-A squares and two matching fabric-B squares for each block as shown in the diagram. (Use the seam allowance marked on the templates throughout.)

98 C-D four-patch blocks: Make 98 C-D four-patch blocks, joining two matching fabric-C squares and two matching fabric-D squares for each block.

TEMPLATES

2½in (6.5cm)
template R

2½in (6.5cm)
template S

5in (13cm)
template T

10in (26cm)
template U

2in (5cm)
template V

Triangle block (inner border)

5in (13cm)

Parallelogram block (inner border)

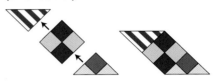

Partial parallelogram block (inner border)

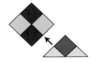

Corner block (inner border)

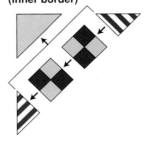

Four-patch block

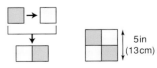

5in (13cm)

Four-triangle block

2in (5cm)

Stitching on corner triangles

Fold a small fabric-X square (one of the 392 squares) in half diagonally and

ASSEMBLY

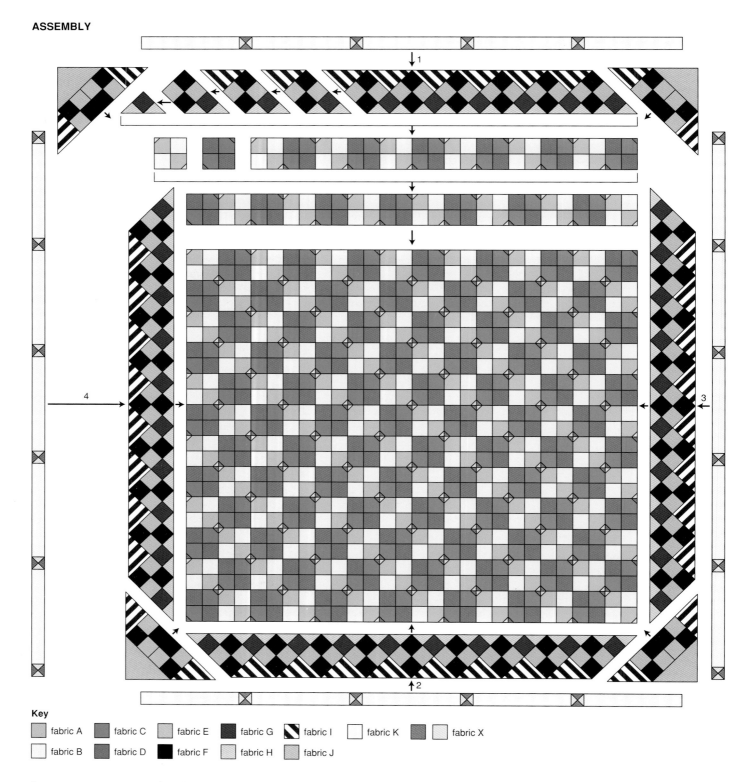

Key

fabric A	fabric C	fabric E	fabric G	fabric I	fabric K	fabric X
fabric B	fabric D	fabric F	fabric H	fabric J		

finger-press to crease the diagonal fold. Unfold the creased square and place it on the outside corner of a fabric-A square on an A-B block, with the right sides facing and the edges aligned. Stitch along the diagonal

crease (see page 80 for a diagram showing how this is done). Trim off the outside triangles ¼in (7.5mm) beyond this new seam. Then press the fabric-X triangle away from the centre of the block. Attach a fabric-X corner

triangle (not a matching patch) to the second fabric-A corner on the same block.
Attach two fabric-X corners to each of the 196 four-patch blocks for the centre quilt, joining them to the fabric-

A patches on the A-B blocks and to the fabric-C patches on the C-D blocks.

Assembling quilt centre

Following the assembly diagram, arrange the 196 blocks for the quilt centre into 14 rows of 14 blocks, alternating the A-B blocks with the C-D blocks and positioning them so that the X-fabric triangles meet in the corners to form tiny squares. Make the arrangement on the floor or on a cotton-flannel design wall (see page 144). Once you have achieved the desired effect, sew the blocks together in rows, then join the rows.

INNER BORDER

Making inner-border blocks

Make the following blocks using the diagrams on page 93 as a guide.

44 E-F four-patch blocks: Make 44 E-F four-patch blocks, joining two matching fabric-E squares and two matching fabric-F squares for each block.

40 G-H triangle blocks: Make 40 G-H triangle blocks, joining two matching fabric-H triangles to a fabric-G square for each triangle block.

32 parallelogram blocks: Make 32 parallelogram blocks, joining one fabric-I triangle and one G-H triangle block to an E-F four-patch block for each parallelogram. (Make sure the stripes on the fabric-I triangles all face in the same direction.)

4 partial parallelogram blocks: Make four partial parallelogram blocks, omitting the fabric-I triangles.

4 corner blocks: Make four corner blocks, each from two E-F four-patch blocks, two fabric-I triangles and one large fabric-J triangle.

Assembling inner border

Arrange eight parallelogram blocks, one partial parallelogram block and one G-H triangle block into a border

to fit along one side of the quilt centre (see diagram) and sew the blocks together.

Arrange and sew together the blocks for the other three sides of the border in the same way. Since there are bias triangle edges on the inner border, pin them to the quilt centre and baste if necessary. Then machine stitch, placing the inner border against the sewing machine feed dogs to help ease in. Next, join the four corner blocks to the corners of the quilt.

OUTER BORDER

Making outer-border blocks

20 fabric-X four-triangle blocks: Make 20 fabric-X four-triangle blocks, joining four non-matching fabric-X triangles for each block.

Assembling outer border

Arrange and join five fabric-K strips and four fabric-X four-triangle blocks – alternating the strips and blocks and beginning and ending with a strip. Join three more outer borders in the same way. Then join an extra four-triangle block to each end of two of the borders. Join the short borders to opposite sides of the quilt, then the long borders; again, baste if necessary and place the inner border bias edges against the feed dogs when stitching.

FINISHING

Press the quilt top. Layer the quilt top, batting and backing; and baste (see page 148).

Using deep blue or deep green thread, machine-quilt as shown in the diagram. Trim the quilt edges. Then cut the fabric-K binding on the bias from fabric K and attach (see page 149).

ALTERNATIVE COLOURWAY

This *Moody Whites* alternative colourway (see page 34) was made to give you an idea of how you can make

Quilting for Moody Blues

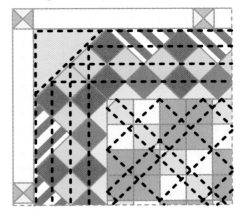

up your own colourway and change the appearance of the patchwork.

Moody Whites

Moody Whites was made in the same way as *Moody Blues*, except that the quilt centre has 12 rows of 12 blocks and a simple 5in (13cm) wide border. The finished quilt measures 70in × 70in (178cm × 178cm).

There are only two fabric groups for the four-patch blocks on the *Moody Whites* quilt – fabric A and fabric B. Each block is made from a pair of fabric-A template-R squares and a pair of fabric-B squares. The corner triangles are usually joined to the pair of paler patches (fabric A) on the block. The overall look is one of very pale, hardly distinguishable tones in dusty, chalky colours.

• **Fabric A:** Predominantly monochromatic solid-looking prints in whites and off-whites

• **Fabric B:** Pale, predominantly monochromatic solid-looking prints in taupes, watered-down siennas and mouldy greens

• **Fabric X:** Light-toned prints in chalky pastel turquoises, blues, limes, dusty rose and butterscotch

• **Border fabric:** Pale sand monochromatic dot print

• **Binding fabric:** Narrow white on white stripe

• **Quilting thread:** Off-white thread

red courthouse steps

The instructions that follow are for the *Red Courthouse Steps* (see also, page 37). Experienced patchworkers might like to try the quilt in an alternative colourway – fabric descriptions for a yellow and an indigo version are given on pages 98 and 99.

SIZE

The finished *Red Courthouse Steps* measures approximately 76in × 76in (190cm × 190cm).

Note that measurements on the diagrams are for finished patch sizes, excluding the seam allowances.

Special note: This pattern is worked in the 'courthouse steps' variation of the traditional 'log cabin' pattern. Each of the four sides of each log cabin block is made of strips of a single fabric, and each of the four sides of the block is different from the other three. Each side is joined to the exact same fabric on a neighbouring block. This makes for a wonderful optical illusion of Chinese-lantern (or stepped-diamond) shapes.

INGREDIENTS

44–45in (112–114cm) wide 100% cotton fabrics:
• **Fabric A:** ¼–½yd (25–46cm) of at least 25 different fabrics, mostly in

medium-scale prints and dots with a few plaids, and predominantly in reds – from clarets, beetroots and burgundys to magentas, scarlets and red-oranges
• **Fabric B:** ½yd (46cm) of KAFFE FASSETT's 'chartreuse' *Shot Cotton* (SC12) in or a similar solid-coloured deep chartreuse fabric
• **Fabric C:** ¼yd (25cm) of KAFFE FASSETT's 'pomegranate' *Shot Cotton*

(SC09) or a similar solid-coloured pomegranate red fabric
• **Fabric D:** 1yd (91cm) of KAFFE FASSETT's 'red' *Roman Glass* (GP01-R) or a similar multi-coloured, mainly red, circles print
• **Backing fabric:** 5yd (4.6m)
• **Binding fabric:** ½yd (46cm) extra of fabric D
• **Wool or thick polyester batting:** 83in × 83in (208cm × 208cm)

Cutting patches in matching fabric sets

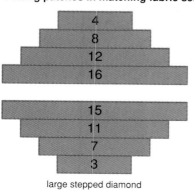

large stepped diamond

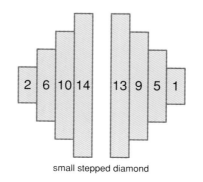

small stepped diamond

Log cabin block

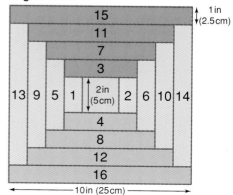

• **Quilting ties:** Embroidery thread in burgundy

CUTTING PATCHES
Quilt centre

Because the patchwork pattern is formed by matching the four fabrics of each log cabin block to the fabrics of neighbouring blocks to form 'stepped diamonds', the patches are cut from the same fabric in a set of strips for each stepped diamond, *rather than in a set for each block*. The stepped diamonds are arranged in rows to form the quilt pattern, then they are divided into sets of strips for sewing into blocks.

42 large stepped diamonds: For each of the 42 large stepped diamonds, cut eight strips from a single fabric A as follows:

ASSEMBLY

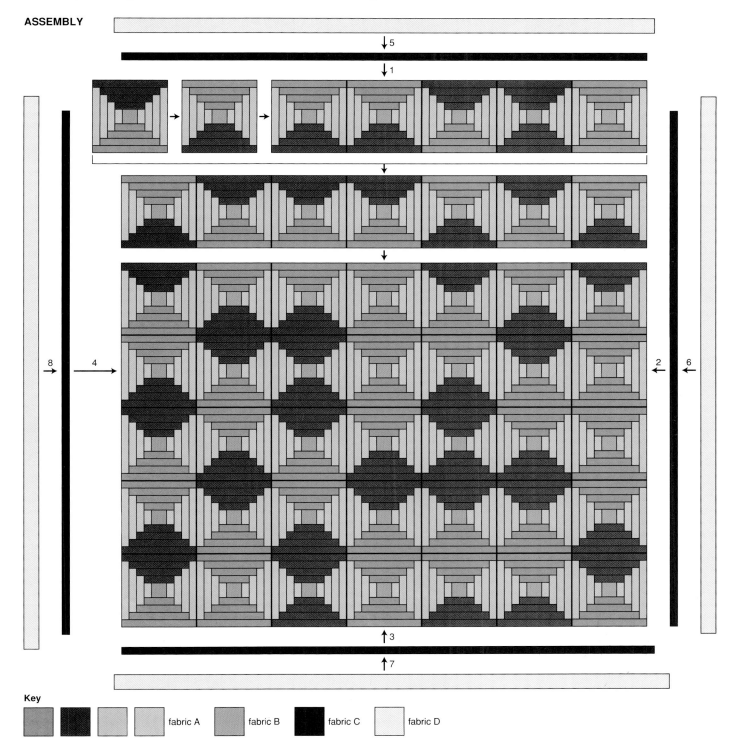

Key

fabric A   fabric B   fabric C   fabric D

- Cut two strips 1½in x 4½in (4cm x 11.5cm) – for *sections 3 and 4* on a log cabin block (see diagrams on page 96).
- Cut two strips 1½in x 6½in (4cm x 16.5cm) – for *sections 7 and 8*.
- Cut two strips 1½in x 8½in (4cm x 21.5cm) – for *sections 11 and 12*.
- Cut two strips 1½in x 10½in (4cm x 26.5cm) – for *sections 15 and 16*.

14 large stepped half-diamonds: For each of the 14 large stepped half-diamonds, cut four strips from a single fabric A – one strip in each of the sizes for the full large diamonds.

42 small stepped diamonds: For each of the 42 small stepped diamonds, cut eight strips from a single fabric A as follows:

- Cut two strips 1½in x 2½in (4cm x 6.5cm) – for *sections 1 and 2* on a log cabin block (see diagrams on page 96).
- Cut two strips 1½in x 4½in (4cm x 11.5cm) – for *sections 5 and 6*.
- Cut two strips 1½in x 6½in (4cm x 16.5cm) – for *sections 9 and 10*.
- Cut two strips 1½in x 8½in (4cm x 21.5cm) – for *sections 13 and 14*.

14 small stepped half-diamonds: For each of the 14 small stepped half-diamonds, cut four strips from a single fabric A – one strip in each of the sizes for the full small diamonds.

49 centre squares for blocks: Cut 49 squares 2½in x 2½in (6.5cm x 6.5cm) from fabric B (chartreuse).

Inner border

4 strips: From fabric C (pomegranate red), cut four strips – one strip 1½in x 70½in (4cm x 176.5cm), two strips 1½in x 71½in (4cm x 179cm) and one strip 1½in x 72½in (4cm x 181.5cm).

Inner border

4 strips: From fabric D (circles print), cut four strips – one strip 2½in x 72½in (6.5cm x 181.5cm), two strips 2½in x 74½in (6.5cm x 186.5cm) and

one strip 2½in x 76½in (6.5cm x 191.5cm).

ARRANGING STEPPED DIAMONDS

Following the assembly diagram, arrange the sets of diamond strips in seven rows of six small stepped diamonds alternating with six rows of seven large stepped diamonds, and fill in the side edges with the small stepped half-diamonds and the top and bottom with the large ones. Make the arrangement on the floor or on a cotton-flannel design wall (see page 144). Then position a chartreuse centre square where the 'points' on the 'diamonds' meet.

MAKING LOG CABIN BLOCKS

49 log cabin blocks: Once you have achieved an arrangement you like, divide the strips into sets of 16 strips for each of the 49 log cabin blocks with the accompanying chartreuse centre square (see the block diagram on page 96), but keeping them laid out in their arrangement.

Pick up a set of 16 patches for the first block. Then using a ¼in (7.5mm) seam allowance throughout, stitch *section 1* to the centre square, then *section 2*, then *section 3*, and so on, following the sequence on the block diagram. Press the seam allowances towards the outside edge as you proceed.

Make the remaining 48 blocks in the same way.

To keep track of the position of each log cabin block, it is a good idea to sew them together in horizontal rows of seven blocks as you make them (see the assembly diagram).

ASSEMBLING QUILT CENTRE

If you haven't already, sew the log cabin blocks together in seven rows,

each seven blocks long, then join the seven horizontal rows together.

ASSEMBLING INNER BORDER

Sew the shortest inner border strip to the top edge of the centre.

Next, sew one of the two medium-length strips to the right side, then the second to the bottom edge.

Finally, sew the longest strip to the left side.

ASSEMBLING OUTER BORDER

Sew on the outer border strips in the same sequence as for the inner border.

FINISHING

Press the quilt top. Layer the quilt top, batting and backing; and baste. 'Quilt' the patchwork together with small burgundy ties (see page 148). Place one tie at the corner of each log cabin block, one halfway between each of these ties, and finally one at each of the corners of the small chartreuse centre square of each block.

Trim the quilt edges. Then cut the binding and attach (see page 149).

ALTERNATIVE COLOURWAYS

Two alternative colourways for this quilt – *Indigo Courthouse Steps* on page 39 and *Yellow Courthouse Steps* on page 38 – were made to give you an idea of how you can make up your own colourway.

Both of the alternative versions are smaller than *Red Courthouse Steps*, so if you'd like attempt one of these versions, remember that you won't need quite as much fabric A as for the red version.

Indigo Courthouse Steps

This quilt is six blocks by six blocks and has a single 5in (13cm) wide border. The finished patchwork

measures 60in (150cm) square.
• **Fabric A:** Dark to medium indigo prints and dots, and a single check (overall effect should be deep)
• **Fabric B:** KAFFE FASSETT's 'chartreuse' *Shot Cotton* (SC12) or a similar solid-coloured deep chartreuse fabric
• **Border fabric:** Dark indigo tie-dye stripe
• **Binding fabric:** Pin dots on navy ground
• **Quilting ties:** Purple embroidery thread

Yellow Courthouse Steps

This quilt is seven blocks by seven blocks and has no border. The individual blocks on this version are made from 12 strips (instead of 16), so they are each 8in (20.5cm) square. The finished patchwork measures 56in (143.5cm) square.

Instead of being tied, the quilt is held together with embroidery stitches (see *Embroidery Threads* below).
• **Fabric A:** Medium-scale prints, dots, plaids and one stripe in hot yellows and golds, with a few lighter yellows
• **Fabric B:** KAFFE FASSETT's 'chartreuse' *Shot Cotton* (SC12) or a similar solid-coloured deep chartreuse fabric
• **Binding fabric:** KAFFE FASSETT's yellow *Pebble Beach* (GP06-C) or a similar toasty yellow print with copper accents
• **Embroidery threads:** Thick twisted silks and/or knitting and embroidery cottons in pinks, blues, greens, yellows, golds and orange. Embroider a flower of two or three concentric rounds of radiating straight stitches on each chartreuse centre square, starting at the middle and leaving a ¾in (2cm) circle of chartreuse fabric visible. Embroider a single orange star stitch in the centre of each of the four sides of each log cabin block and seed stitches in the chartreuse centres of the flowers.

nona

Keep the palette for the free-form log cabin blocks on this patchwork high and clear with only a couple of dustier antique notes such as grey-blue or wine (see pages 40 and 41 for more about *Nona*).

SIZE

The finished patchwork measures approximately 65½in × 85¼in (166.5cm × 216.5cm).
Note that any measurements on the diagrams are for finished patch sizes, excluding the seam allowances.

INGREDIENTS

44–45in (112–114cm) wide 100% cotton fabrics:
• **Log cabin patch fabric:** ¼yd (25cm) each of at least five different yellows, and ¼yd (25cm) each of an assortment of oranges, wines, acid greens, turquoises and warm and cool shades of lavender, all predominantly in monochromatic prints, plus a few solids and multi-coloured prints

ASSEMBLY

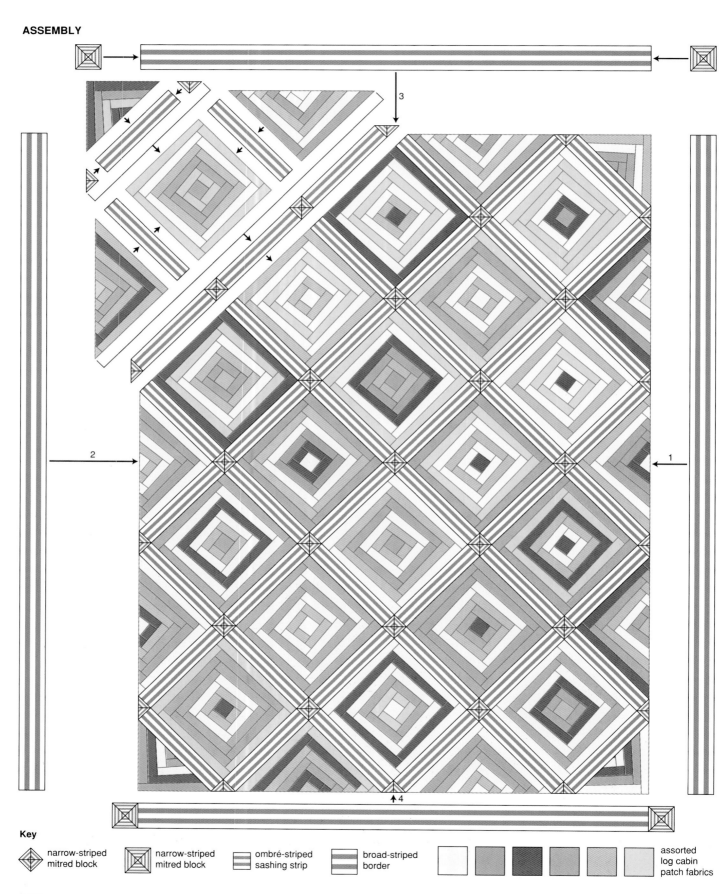

Key

◈ narrow-striped mitred block

⊠ narrow-striped mitred block

▤ ombré-striped sashing strip

▥ broad-striped border

▢ ▨ ▨ ▨ ▨ ▨ assorted log cabin patch fabrics

TEMPLATES

2in (5cm)
template V

3in (7.5cm)
template X

Free-form log cabin block

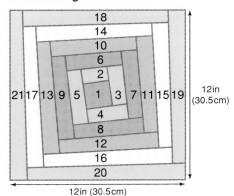

• **Mitred-block fabric:** ½yd (46cm) of KAFFE FASSETT's narrow *Blue and White Stripe* (BWS01) or a similar narrow, dusty blue and ecru stripe

• **Sashing-strip fabric:** ½yd (46cm) of KAFFE FASSETT's blue *Ombré Stripe* (OS02) or a similar blue and ecru ombré stripe

• **Border fabric:** 1½yd (1.4m) of KAFFE FASSETT's broad *Blue and White Stripe* (BWS02) or a similar broad, dusty blue and ecru stripe fabric (see binding)

• **Backing fabric:** 5yd (4.6m)

• **Binding fabric:** ¾yd (70cm) extra of border fabric

• **Lightweight cotton batting:** 73in × 93in (185cm × 235cm)

• **Quilting thread:** Ecru thread

• **Templates:** Use templates V and X on page 153 for mitred blocks, and make your own templates for trimming the log cabin blocks as explained below

CUTTING PATCHES
Quilt centre

Log cabin patches: From assorted log cabin patch fabrics, cut 25 patches about 2–3in (5–8cm) square, cutting freehand by eye so they aren't exact

squares. Then cut the remaining log cabin patch fabrics into long strips 1½in–2½in (4–6.5cm) wide (the sides of the strip should be straight but don't have to be absolutely parallel). You can start out with a few long strips cut from each of your assorted fabrics, then cut more as you need them when stitching the free-form log cabin blocks.

17 small mitred blocks: From the narrow, blue and ecru stripe fabric, cut 68 template-V triangles, cutting the patches so that the stripes run parallel to the longest side of the template. (The stripes on the triangles don't have to match exactly.)

14 small mitred half blocks: From the narrow, blue and ecru stripe fabric, cut 28 template-V triangles in the same way as for the full mitred block triangles.

48 sashing strips: From the blue ombré stripe fabric, cut 48 sashing strips 2½in × 12½in (6.5cm × 31.5cm), cutting the patches so that the stripes run lengthways along the strips.

Border

Border strips: From the broad, blue and ecru stripe fabric, cut two strips 3½in × 79¾in (9cm × 202.5cm) and two strips 3½in × 60in (9cm × 152.5cm).

4 mitred corner blocks: Cut 16 template-X triangles from the narrow, blue and ecru stripe fabric in the same way as for the small mitred block triangles.

MAKING BLOCK TEMPLATES

The log cabin blocks on this quilt are cut and pieced freehand, so the strips ('logs') are not absolutely rectangular. The irregular pieced blocks are made to a larger size than required, then pressed and trimmed into perfect squares. (The log cabin triangle blocks are also first trimmed into perfect squares and then folded in half diagonally and bisected.)

To cut perfect squares from the finished blocks, you will need cardboard templates to trace around, or paper pattern shapes to pin on and

cut around. Draw the template squares on sewing pattern paper (or other graph paper) and use them like this, or glue them to stiff cardboard if you want to trace around them. All the template dimensions below include the seam allowances.

For the log cabin blocks: Make a square template 12½in × 12½in (31.5cm × 31.5cm).

For the log cabin edge triangles: Make a square template 12⅞in × 12⅞in (32.5cm × 32.5cm).

For the log cabin corner triangles: Make a square template 9⅜in × 9⅜in (24cm × 24cm).

Label the templates and set them aside until you're ready to trim the pieced log cabin blocks.

QUILT CENTRE
Making blocks

25 log cabin blocks: Make 25 free-form log cabin blocks, following the diagram for the sequence and using a ¼in (7.5mm) seam allowance throughout.

To begin each block, select one of the log cabin centre squares (*patch 1*). Then cut a short strip (*patch 2*) from one of the contrasting log cabin patch fabrics prepared earlier, cutting it a little longer than the top of the square. Place *patch 2* on top of *patch 1* with the right sides facing and the raw edges aligned along the top of the square. Sew the patches together along the aligned edges. Then open out the joined patches so that they are both right side up, and press. With *patch 2* at the top, trim the right side-edge of *patch 2* to straighten it and to align it with the side edge of the centre square. With the joined patches still right side up, place another strip of the same fabric (*patch 3*) face down on the joined patches and align it with the edge just trimmed. Sew

patch 3 in place along this edge. Open so that the joined patches are all right side up, and press. Add two more strips in the same fabric (*patches 4 and 5*) and in the same way, working clockwise around the centre square. Then add four more rings of colour as shown on the diagram, using a different contrasting fabric for each ring of strips.

The final block should be 13½–14in (34–36cm) square, so add an extra ring if required, or add fewer rings if you have reached the approximate finished size sooner – but always end with a complete ring of colour. (If desired, you can press and trim your first completed block, as explained below, before proceeding, just to check that your free-form strips are working.)

17 small mitred blocks: Make 17 small mitred blocks, joining four striped template-V triangles for each block as shown in the diagram for the *Optical Squares Tablecloth* on page 128. Use the seam allowance marked on the templates. (The stripes on the triangles don't have to match exactly.)

14 small mitred half blocks: Make 14 small mitred half blocks, joining two striped template-V triangles for each half block.

Trimming log cabin blocks

18 whole log cabin blocks: Choose 18 of the finished log cabin blocks for the whole blocks in the centre, then press and trim them to 12½in × 12½in (31.5cm × 31.5cm), using your template.

10 log cabin edge triangles: Choose five of the remaining log cabin blocks for the edge triangles, then press and trim them to 12⅞in × 12⅞in (32.5cm × 32.5cm), using your template. Fold each of these blocks in half diagonally and bisect to make a total of 10 triangles.

4 log cabin corner triangles: Use the two remaining log cabin blocks for the corner triangles, then press and trim them to 9⅜in × 9⅜in (24cm × 24cm), using your template. Fold each of these blocks in half diagonally and bisect to make four triangles. (The corner triangles are not 'on point' like the rest of the blocks in the quilt.)

Assembling quilt centre

Following the assembly diagram, arrange the log cabin blocks, sashing strips and small mitred blocks on the floor or on a cotton-flannel design wall (see page 144). Once you have achieved the desired effect, sew the blocks and strips together in diagonal rows, then join the rows.

BORDER
Making blocks

4 mitred corner blocks: Make four mitred corner blocks, joining four striped template-X triangles for each block as for the small mitred blocks.

Assembling border

Sew a long striped border strip to each of the two sides of the quilt centre. Sew a mitred corner block to each end of each of the two remaining border strips, then join the strips to the top and bottom of the quilt.

FINISHING

Press the quilt top. Layer the quilt top, batting and backing; and baste (see page 148). Using ecru thread and starting at the centre, machine-quilt a squared-off, free-form spiral in each log cabin block and in each sashing square. Along the striped sashing and border strips, machine-quilt a two free-form parallel lines. Around the sashing strips and between the border and quilt centre, machine stitch in-the-ditch. Trim the quilt edges. Then cut the striped binding fabric on the bias and attach (see page 149).

squares window blind

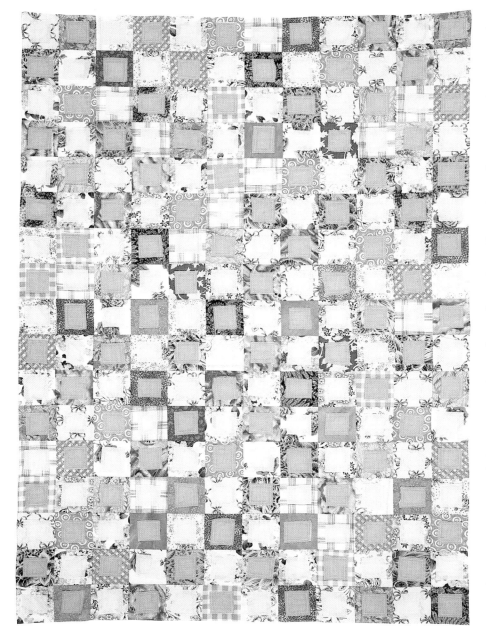

When choosing fabrics for this window blind patchwork, be sure to stick to colours that are very 'dusty' – stay away from anything bright.

SIZE
The finished patchwork measures approximately 36in x 51in (90cm x 127.5cm). *Note that any measurements on the diagrams are for finished patch sizes, excluding the seam allowances.*

INGREDIENTS
44–45in (112–114cm) wide 100% cotton fabrics:
• **Fabric A:** ⅛–¼yd (12–25cm) each of at least six different pale blue-and-white and pale lilac-and-white fabrics, predominantly in delicate small-scale to medium-scale floral prints, and one or two fine-lined plaids
• **Fabric B:** ⅛–¼yd (12–25cm) each of at least 10 different small-scale to medium-scale monochromatic prints in light to medium tones of blue-greens, lavenders, greys, melons and soft reds
• **Fabric C:** ½yd (46cm) of KAFFE FASSETT's 'blush' *Shot Cotton* (SC28) or a similar solid-coloured very pale peach fabric
• **Fabric D:** ½yd (46cm) of KAFFE FASSETT's 'ecru' *Shot Cotton* (SC24) or a similar solid-coloured light putty fabric
• **Topstitching thread:** Ecru sewing machine thread
• **Template:** Use template W on page 152

CUTTING PATCHES
102 fabric-A squares: Cut 102 template-W squares from fabric A.
102 fabric-B squares: Cut 102 template-W squares from fabric B.
102 small fabric-C freehand 'squares': Cutting freehand, cut 102 patches measuring approximately 1¾–2in (4.5–5cm) square from fabric C. (These are not meant to be exact squares, so be sure to cut them freehand.)
102 small fabric-D freehand 'squares': Cutting freehand, cut 102 patches measuring approximately 1¾–2in (4.5–5cm) square from fabric D.

MAKING BLOCKS
102 A-C blocks: Make 102 blocks, machine topstitching one small fabric-C freehand 'square' to the centre of the right side of one fabric-A template-W square for each block as shown in the diagram (without turning under the raw edge of the small freehand square). Using ecru thread,

TEMPLATE

3in (7.5cm)
template W

ASSEMBLY

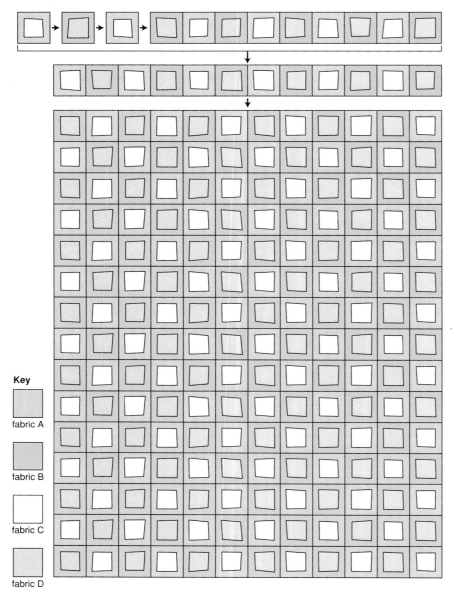

Key

fabric A

fabric B

fabric C

fabric D

Block with topstitched square

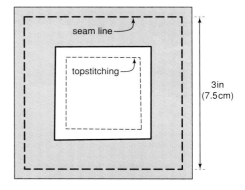

seam line

topstitching

3in
(7.5cm)

about a ¼in (6mm) seam allowance on the wrong side of the block.

ASSEMBLING PATCHWORK

Following the assembly diagram, arrange the blocks into 17 rows of 12 blocks, with the fabric-A and fabric-B blocks alternating. Arrange them on the floor or on a cotton-flannel design wall (see page 144). Once you have achieved the desired effect, sew the blocks together in rows. (Use the seam allowance marked on the templates throughout.) Press the seams open, on the rows of blocks, then join the rows. Again, press the seams open.

Do not trim the thread ends hanging from the seams too much. The patchwork should have a slightly 'shabby' and feathery-light appearance.

topstitch about ¼in (6mm) from the raw edge of the small square, stitching 'free style' without measuring for accuracy.

102 B-D blocks: Make 102 blocks as for the A-C blocks, but using a fabric-B template-W square and a small fabric-D freehand 'square' for each block.

Press each of the finished blocks carefully.

Then cut away the backing fabric (fabric A or B) behind the small centre square on each block, leaving

FINISHING

Turn ¼in (6mm) to the wrong side all around the outer edge of the patchwork and topstitch in place.

To make four hanging tabs for the patchwork, first cut four 2in x 8in (5cm x 20cm) strips from fabric C or D. Fold each strip in half lengthways aligning the raw edges. Stitch along the long side ¼in (6mm) from the edge. Turn right side out and press. Fold each tab strip in half widthways and sew them, evenly spaced, to the wrong side of the top of the blind.

fonthill quilt

These instructions are for the *Fonthill Quilt* (see page 108). Experienced patchworkers might like to try the alternative colourway given on page 109, or their own colour scheme.

SIZE

The finished *Fonthill Quilt* measures approximately 72in × 78in (183cm × 198cm). *Note that any measurements on the diagrams are for finished patch sizes, excluding the seam allowances.*

Special note: There is a very low contrast of tone on the *Fonthill Quilt*, so when 'lighter-toned' (fabrics A and C) and 'darker-toned' (fabrics B and D) patches are referred to, remember that the contrast in tone is minimal.

INGREDIENTS

44–45in (112–114cm) wide 100% cotton fabrics in mostly mini-scale prints, dots, plaids and stripes, plus some solids:

• **Fabric A:** ½yd (46cm) each of at least six different fabrics in *light-medium to medium tones* of dull taupes, toasts, greys, greiges, khakis, olives and rusts
• **Fabric B:** ¼yd (25cm) each of at least different 12 fabrics in *medium to dark-medium tones* of cobalts, olives, greys, grey blues and turquoises
• **Fabric C:** ⅛yd (15cm) each of at least four different fabrics in *light-medium to medium tones* of oranges and pumpkins
• **Fabric D:** ¼yd (25cm) each of at least six different fabrics in *medium to dark-medium tones* of plums, roses and magentas
• **Fabric E:** 1yd (91cm) of an olive tie-dyed batik with flashes of magenta, turquoise and grey-blue
• **Fabric F:** ¾yd (70cm) of a print of olive pin dots on a charcoal ground
• **Backing fabric:** 5yd (4.6m)

• **Binding fabric:** ¾yd (70cm) of KAFFE FASSETT's *Broad Stripe*-BS06, or a similar dark multi-coloured broad stripe, for a bias binding
• **Cotton batting:** 79in × 85in (201cm × 216cm)
• **Quilting thread:** Drab olive-brown thread
• **Templates:** Use templates M, N and O on pages 153 and 157

CUTTING PATCHES

The patch cutting instructions follow the order of the quilt assembly, but it is a good idea to cut the fabric-D triangles for *border 2* and *border 5* first, so that you can use the remainder of fabric D for the rest of the quilt.

Quilt centre
180 small two-tone squares: For the 180 small two-tone squares, cut 180 template-M triangles from fabrics A and C (slightly lighter tones), and 180 template-M triangles from fabrics B and D (slightly darker tones), for a total of 360 triangles.

Border 1
4 strips: Cut two strips 4½in × 30½in (11.5cm × 77.5cm) and two strips 4½in × 24½in (11.5cm × 62cm) from fabric E.
4 large two-tone squares: Cut four large template-N triangles from fabric E and four from fabric F.

Border 2
70 small two-tone squares: Cut 70 template-M triangles from fabric D and 70 from fabric F.
4 corner squares: Cut four template-O squares from fabric E.

Border 3
38 pinwheels: For each of the 38 pinwheels, cut *two sets* of four matching template-M triangles – one set from a single fabric A (slightly lighter tones) and one set from a single fabric B (slightly darker tones).
2 half-pinwheels: For each of the two half-pinwheels, cut *two sets* of two

matching template-M triangles – one set from a single fabric A and one set from a single fabric B.
4 large two-tone squares: Cut four large template-N triangles from fabric E and four from fabric F.

Border 4
4 strips: Cut two strips 4½in × 42½in (11.5cm × 108cm) and two strips 4½in × 36½in (11.5cm × 93cm) from fabric E.
12 large two-tone squares: Cut 12 large template-N triangles from fabric E and 12 from fabric F.

Border 5
110 small two-tone squares: Cut 110 template-M triangles from fabric D and 110 from fabric F.
4 corner squares: Cut four template-O squares fabric E.

Border 6
132 pinwheels: For each of the 132 pinwheels, cut *two sets* of four matching template-M triangles – one set from a single fabric A (slightly lighter tones) and one set from a single fabric B (slightly darker tones).

TEMPLATES

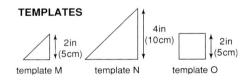

template M   template N   template O

Two-tone square

2in (5cm)

Pinwheel

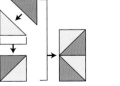 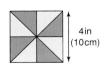

4in (10cm)

4 half-pinwheels: For each of the four half-pinwheels, cut *two sets* of two matching template-M triangles – one set from a single fabric A and one set from a single fabric B.

ASSEMBLY 1

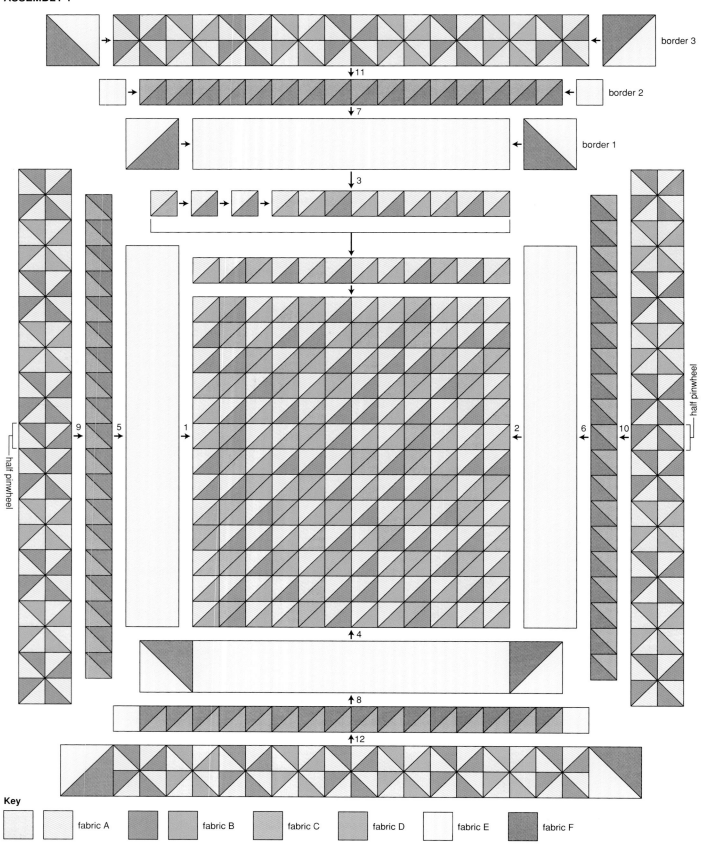

Key

fabric A   fabric B   fabric C   fabric D   fabric E   fabric F

ASSEMBLY 2

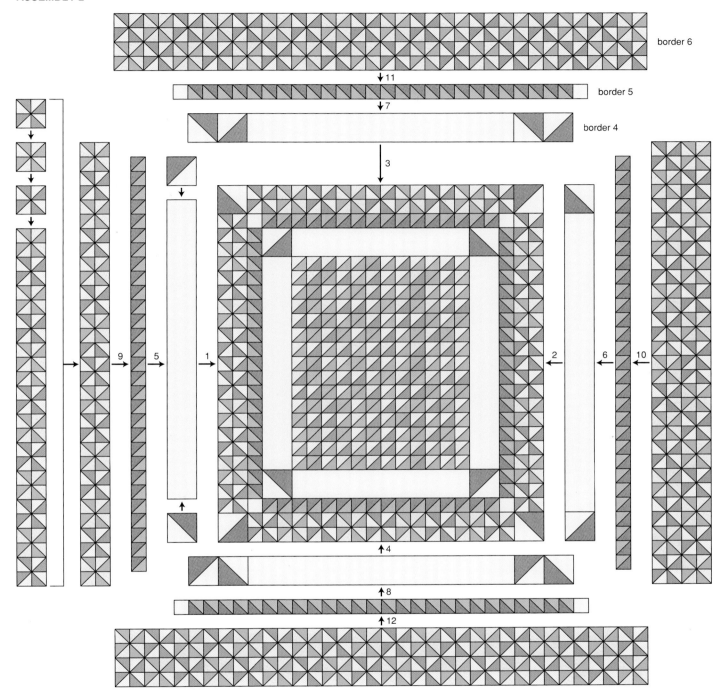

QUILT CENTRE
Making blocks

180 small two-tone squares: Make 180 small two-tone squares, joining one lighter-toned triangle (fabric A or C) to one darker-toned triangle (fabric B or D) for each square as shown in the diagram. (Use the seam allowance marked on the templates throughout.)

Assembling quilt centre

Following the first assembly diagram, arrange the squares into 15 rows of 12 squares. Arrange them on the floor or on a cotton-flannel design wall (see page 144). All the lighter-toned triangles should point in one direction and all the darker-toned triangles in the other. Once you have achieved the

desired effect, sew the blocks together in rows, then join the rows.

BORDERS

When assembling each of the six borders, be sure to follow the assembly diagrams for the positioning of the two-tone squares (in the strips and at the corners) so that the triangles

point in the correct directions.

Making blocks for border 1

4 large two-tone squares: Make four large two-tone squares, joining one fabric-E triangle to one fabric-F triangle for each square as shown in the diagram.

Assembling border 1

Sew one of the longer fabric-E strips to each of the two sides of the quilt centre. For the top and bottom borders, join one large two-tone square to each end of the shorter fabric-E strips, then stitch to the quilt.

Making blocks for border 2

70 small two-tone squares: Make 70 small two-tone squares, joining one fabric-D triangle to one fabric-F triangle for each square.

Assembling border 2

For each of the two side borders, join

19 two-tone squares together in a long strip, then sew to the quilt. For both the top and bottom borders, join 16 two-tone squares and sew a fabric-E square patch to each end of the strip. Stitch to the quilt.

Making blocks for border 3

38 pinwheels: Make 38 pinwheels, joining the eight patches cut for each pinwheel (four matching fabric-A triangles and four matching fabric-B triangles) as shown in the diagram. (Make sure that most of the pinwheels 'spin' in the same direction by placing the darker-toned triangles in the same positions.)

2 half-pinwheels: Make two half-pinwheels, joining the four patches cut for each half-pinwheel (two matching fabric-A triangles and two matching fabric-B triangles).

4 large two-tone squares: Make four large two-tone squares, joining one fabric-E triangle to one fabric-F triangle.

Assembling border 3

For each of the two side borders, join 10 pinwheels and one half-pinwheel together in a long strip, positioning the half pinwheel near the centre of the strip. Sew these to the sides of the quilt.

For both the top and bottom borders, join nine pinwheels and sew a large two-tone square to each end. Stitch the top and bottom borders to the quilt.

Making blocks for border 4

12 large two-tone squares: Make 12 large two-tone squares, joining one fabric-E triangle to one fabric-F triangle for each square as shown in the diagram.

Assembling border 4

For the two sides, join one large two-tone square to each end of the longer fabric-E strips, then stitch to the quilt. For the top and bottom borders, join two large two-tone squares to each

end of the shorter fabric-E strips, then stitch to the quilt.

Making blocks for border 5

110 small two-tone squares: Make 110 small two-tone squares, joining one fabric-D triangle to one fabric-F triangle for each square.

Assembling border 5

For each of the two side borders, join 29 two-tone squares together in a long strip, then sew to the quilt. For both the top and bottom borders, join 26 two-tone squares and sew a fabric-E square patch to each end of the strip. Stitch the top and bottom borders to the quilt.

Making blocks for border 6

132 pinwheels: Make 132 pinwheels, joining the eight patches cut for each pinwheel (four matching fabric-A triangles and four matching fabric-B triangles) as shown in the diagram.

4 half-pinwheels: Make four half-pinwheels, joining the four patches cut for each half-pinwheel (two matching fabric-A triangles and two matching fabric-B triangles).

Assembling border 6

For the two side borders, make a total of four long strips by joining 15 pinwheels and one half-pinwheel, positioning the half-pinwheel near the centre of the strip. Then for each of the borders, join two strips together. Sew these double rows of pinwheels to the sides of the quilt.

For the top and bottom borders, make a total of four long strips by joining 18 pinwheels together. Then for each of the borders, join two strips together and stitch to the quilt.

FINISHING

Press the quilt top. Layer the quilt top, batting and backing; and baste (see page 148).

Using drab olive brown thread, machine-quilt the entire patchwork

with meandering lichen shapes. Trim the quilt edges. Then cut the striped binding fabric on the bias and attach (see page 149).

ALTERNATIVE COLOURWAY

Haitian Fonthill (page 47) is made in the same way as the *Fonthill Quilt* except that the fabric tone groups are different. For *Haitian Fonthill*, cut a total of 180 triangles from fabric B (medium to dark-medium tones) and 180 triangles from a mixture of fabrics A, C and D (pale and light tones). Then when making the two-tone squares, pair a fabric-B patch with a fabric-A, fabric-C or fabric-D patch.

As for the main quilt, the *Haitian Fonthill* uses mostly mini-scale prints, dots, plaids and stripes, plus some solids.

Haitian Fonthill

• **Fabric A:** ½yd (46cm) each of at least six different fabrics in light tones of pinks, salmons and roses
• **Fabric B:** ¼yd (25cm) each of at least 14 different fabrics in medium to dark-medium tones of sea blues, sea greens, emeralds, turquoises and grey blues
• **Fabric C:** ⅛yd (15cm) each of at least four different fabrics in light tones of chartreuses and pale tones of acid yellow-greens
• **Fabric D:** ¼yd (25cm) each of at least six different fabrics in pale tones of pinks
• **Fabric E:** 1yd (91cm) of KAFFE FASSETT'S 'stone' *Gazania* (GP03-S) or a similar large-scale floral print in muted lilacs, ochres and olives on a taupe ground
• **Fabric F:** ¾yd (70cm) of medium-scale monochromatic print in mid blue-greens
• **Binding fabric:** ¾yd (70cm) of a light green and lilac plaid for bias binding
• **Quilting thread:** Light grey-green thread (machine-quilt in meandering palm-leaf shapes)

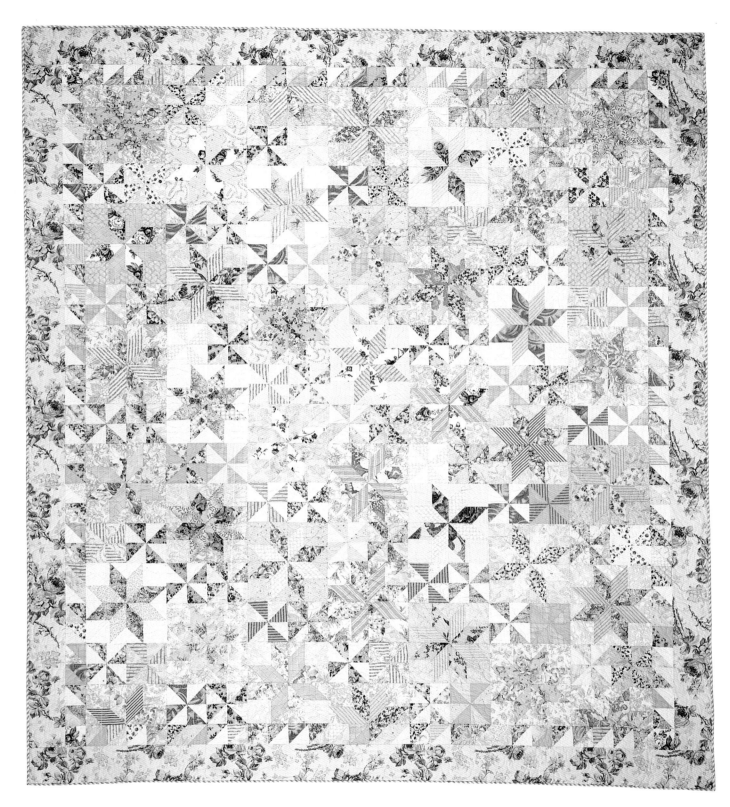

wedding quilt

There is very little tone contrast on the pale prints in this quilt, so the overall effect is of 'faded' colours.

SIZE

The finished patchwork measures approximately 101in × 113in (257cm × 287cm).

Note that any measurements on the *diagrams are for finished patch sizes,* *excluding the seam allowances.*

Special note: The colouring on this quilt is very subtle. Fabric C (the

TEMPLATES

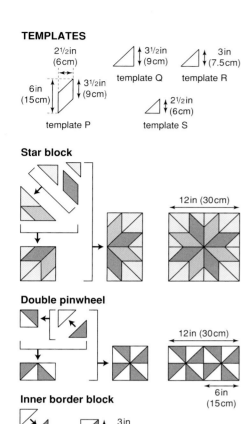

Star block

12in (30cm)

Double pinwheel

12in (30cm)

6in (15cm)

Inner border block

3in (7.5cm)

assortment of 'background' fabrics) on the double pinwheels and on the inner border blocks is mostly whites and off-whites, while fabric C on the star blocks is mostly whites faintly tinged with beige, pink and green. But this distinction is very subtle and not totally consistent.

INGREDIENTS

44–45in (112–114cm) wide 100% cotton fabrics:

• **Fabric A:** Scraps of an assortment of prints, florals and narrow stripes in pastel rose pinks

• **Fabric B:** Scraps of an assortment of prints, florals and narrow stripes in pastel blues and pastel blue-greens

• **Fabric C ('backgrounds'):** Scraps of solids, prints and narrow stripes in whites, off-whites and whites faintly tinged with beige, pink and green

• **Fabric D (outer border):** 3¼yd (3m) of a large-scale faded floral print with

pink roses on a deep cream ground

• **Backing fabric:** 9yd (8.3m)

• **Binding fabric:** 1yd (91cm) of a narrow pink-and-white stripe for a bias binding

• **Cotton batting:** 108in × 120in (275cm × 305cm)

• **Quilting thread:** Off-white thread

• **Templates:** Use templates P, Q, R and S on page 150

CUTTING PATCHES
Quilt centre

35 star blocks: For each of the 35 star blocks, cut *two sets* of four matching template-P diamonds (a total of 8 diamonds for each block), using a single fabric A for one set and a single fabric B for the other; or use two A fabrics or two B fabrics. (When cutting stripes, pay attention to the direction of the stripes on these star points.) Then from a single fabric C ('background' fabric), cut eight template-Q triangles and eight template-S triangles for each block.

5 half-star blocks: For each of the five half-star blocks, cut *two sets* of two matching template-P diamonds (a total of 4 diamonds for each block), using a single fabric A for one set and a single fabric B for the other set; or use two A fabrics or two B fabrics. Then from a single fabric C ('background' fabric), cut four template-Q triangles and four template-S triangles for each block.

74 pinwheels: For each of the 74 pinwheels, cut *two sets* of four matching template-R triangles – one set from a single fabric A and one set from a single fabric C.

Inner border

120 inner border blocks: For the 120 inner border blocks, cut 120 template-R triangles from an assortment of A fabrics and 120 template-R triangles from an assortment of C fabrics.

4 corner squares: From a single

fabric-A floral, cut four squares 3½in × 3½in (9cm × 9cm).

Outer border

4 outer border strips: From fabric D, cut two strips 6in × 102½in (15cm × 260cm) and two strips 6in × 101½in (15cm × 258cm).

QUILT CENTRE
Making blocks

35 star blocks: Make 35 star blocks, joining the patches cut for each block as shown in the diagram. (Use the seam allowance marked on the templates throughout.)

5 half-star blocks: Make 5 half-star blocks, joining the patches cut for each block.

37 double pinwheels: Make 37 double pinwheels, first making 74 pinwheels using the patches cut for each pinwheel, then joining the pinwheels into pairs as shown in the diagram, using two different pinwheels for each pair.

Assembling quilt centre

Following the assembly diagram, arrange the blocks in seven vertical rows on the floor or on a cotton-flannel design wall (see page 144 for how to make a design wall from two large boards). Once you have achieved the desired effect, sew the blocks together in rows, then join the rows.

BORDERS
Making blocks for inner border

120 inner border blocks: Make 120 inner border blocks, joining a fabric A triangle and a fabric C triangle for each block as shown in the diagram.

Assembling inner border

For both the top and bottom borders, join 28 blocks together in a long strip and sew to the quilt centre. For each of the two side borders, join 32 blocks together, then sew a floral corner square to each end. Stitch the side borders to the quilt.

ASSEMBLY

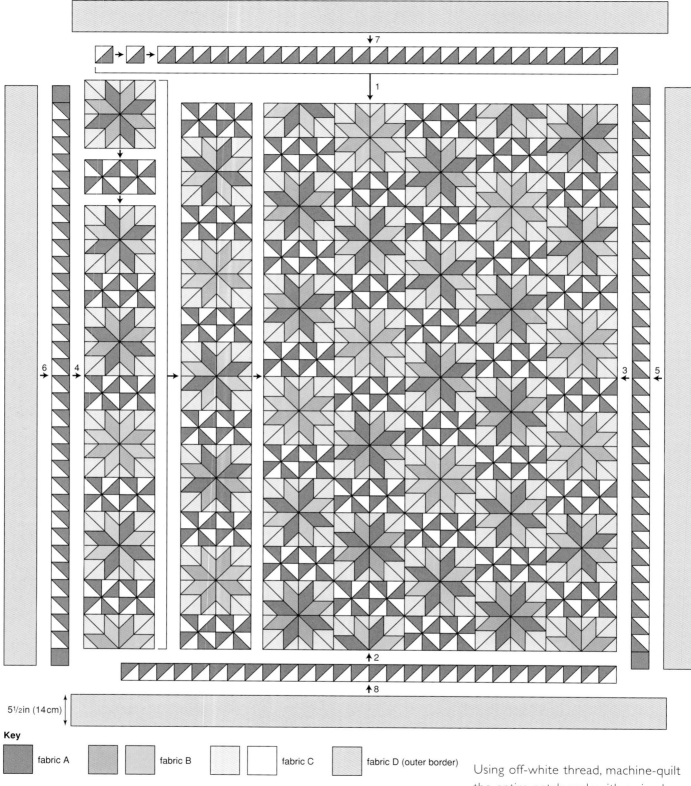

5¹/₂in (14cm)

Key

fabric A   fabric B   fabric C   fabric D (outer border)

Assembling outer border

Sew the longer strips to the sides of
the quilt, then sew the shorter strips
to the top and bottom.

FINISHING

Press the quilt top. Layer the quilt top,
batting and backing; and baste (see
page 148).

Using off-white thread, machine-quilt
the entire patchwork with a simple,
curving, floral-shape repeat.
Then trim the quilt edges, cut the
striped binding fabric on the bias and
attach (see page 149).

delft baskets

The 'flowers' in the baskets on the *Delft Baskets* patchwork are cut from two different KAFFE FASSETT *Pressed Roses* prints. If you are choosing your own fabrics for them, try to find at least two similar simple two-tone prints in dark blue and white or ecru. The instructions are for the *Delft Baskets* (see page 115), and an alternative colourway, in earthy autumn shades, is given at the end.

SIZE

The finished *Delft Baskets* measures approximately 59in × 59in (150cm × 150cm).

Note that any measurements on the diagrams are for finished patch sizes, excluding the seam allowances.

INGREDIENTS

44–45in (112–114cm) wide 100% cotton fabrics:

• **Fabric A (basket fabric):** ½yd (46cm) each of at least three different inky deep blue fabrics in small-scale prints or plaids (choose prints that have a 'woven' effect as this will make the patches look more like baskets)

• **Fabric B:** 1yd (91cm) of KAFFE FASSETT'S *Pressed Roses*-PR03 or a similar bicolour print with white flowers on an indigo ground (see binding fabric), and ½yd (46cm) of *Pressed Roses*-PR07 or a similar bicolour print with off-white flowers on a cobalt ground

• **Fabric C:** ¼yd (25cm) each of at least eight different two-tone fabrics in light blues combined with beige or cream, and in light toasty browns combined with pale beige – all in stripes, plaids and small-scale prints

• **Fabric D:** ¼yd (25cm) each of at least eight different dark blue fabrics in monochromatic or two-tone small-scale or medium-scale florals

• **Fabric E:** ½yd (46cm) of KAFFE FASSETT'S 'ecru' *Shot Cotton* (SC24) or a similar solid-coloured light putty fabric

• **Backing fabric:** 3yd (2.8m)

• **Binding fabric:** ½yd (46cm) extra of KAFFE FASSETT'S *Pressed Roses*-PR03 or a similar bicolour print with white flowers on an indigo ground

• **Lightweight cotton batting:** 66in × 66in (168cm × 168cm)

• **Quilting thread:** Medium blue thread

• **Templates:** Use templates O, Y, Q and R on pages 153 and 157

CUTTING PATCHES

Quilt centre

25 basket blocks: For the 25 basket blocks, cut 25 template-Y triangles from fabric A, and 25 template-Y triangles from fabric B (cutting about half from each of the two B fabrics).

460 checkerboard squares: For the checkerboard background, cut 208 template-O squares from fabric C and 252 template-O squares from fabric D.

Border

156 border squares: Cut 76 template-O squares from fabric E, and 80 template-O squares from the remaining fabric B (the 'indigo' colourway).

80 edging triangles: Cut 80 template-Q triangles from fabric E.

4 corner triangles: Cut 4 template-R triangles from fabric E.

MAKING BLOCKS

25 basket blocks: Make 25 basket blocks, joining one fabric-A and one fabric-B template-Y triangle for each block as shown in the diagram above right. (Use the seam allowance marked on the templates throughout.)

ASSEMBLING PATCHWORK

Following the assembly diagram on page 114, arrange the fabric-C and

TEMPLATES

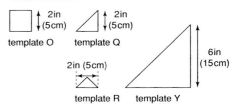

Basket blocks

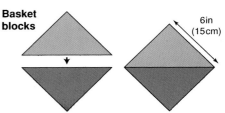

fabric-D squares and the basket blocks in diagonal rows on the floor or on a cotton-flannel design wall (see page 144). Make sure the light and dark squares of the checkerboard background alternate correctly – the placement of these squares is tricky, and it is easy to be 'off' by one square.

Once you have achieved the desired effect, arrange the border around the edge. Sew the patches and blocks together in diagonal rows, then join the rows.

FINISHING

Press the quilt top. Layer the quilt top, batting and backing; and baste (see page 148).

Using medium blue thread, machine-quilt the basket blocks as shown in the diagram. Machine-quilt the checkerboard background and the border in meandering squiggles.

Trim the quilt edges. Then cut the binding and attach (see page 149).

ALTERNATIVE COLOURWAY

Citrus Baskets (page 53) is made entirely from KAFFE FASSETT quilting fabrics (see page 159). The finished quilt measures approximately 54in (137cm) square.

If you are an experienced

patchworker and want to make this quilt, follow the main instructions but eliminate the border, which includes one row of squares in fabric-E squares and one row of squares in fabric-B. Instead, cut 76 template-Q edging triangles and 4 template-R corner triangles from fabric C.

ASSEMBLY

Citrus Baskets Throw

- **Fabric A (basket fabric):** ½yd (46cm) each of four different KAFFE FASSETT stripes, or similar multi-coloured stripes, in mostly reds and oranges
- **Fabric B:** ¼yd (25cm) each of at least six different KAFFE FASSETT prints, or similar medium- and large-scale prints, predominantly in yellows and ochres (we used *Artichokes* GP07-L and GP07-J, *Gazania* GP03-C, *Pressed*

Quilting for Delft Baskets

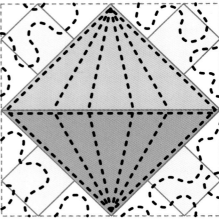

Key

fabric A

fabric B

fabric C

fabric D

fabric E

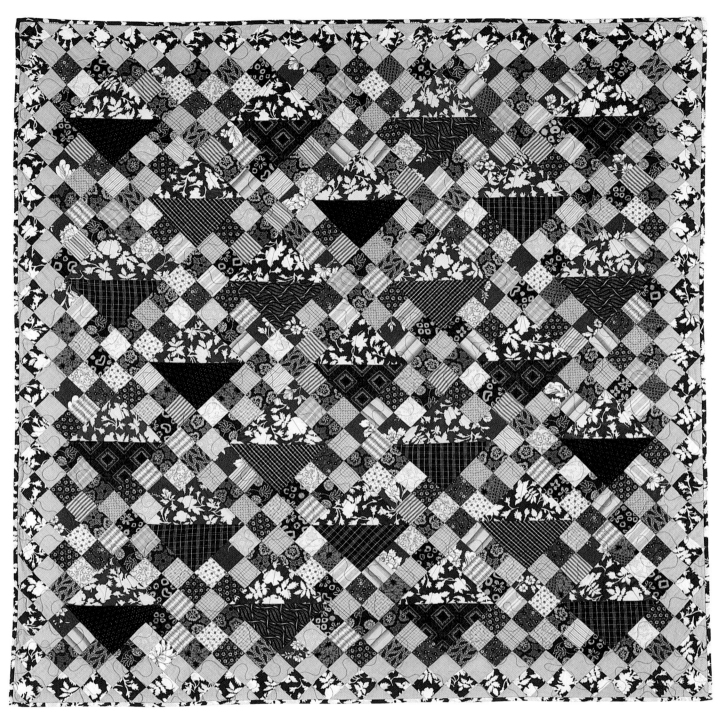

Roses PR02, *Pebble Beach* GP06-J and GP06-C, and *Chard* GP09-C)
• **Fabric C:** Total of 2yd (1.9m) of an assortment of KAFFE FASSETT *Shot Cottons* or similar solid-coloured fabrics, in olives, dusty oranges, rusts and mid browns (we used SC01, SC11, SC12, SC18 and SC16)
• **Fabric D:** Total of 2yd (1.9m) of an

assortment of at least five different KAFFE FASSETT prints, or similar medium-scale prints, in medium-toned greens, green-blues, olives, ochres and hot reds (we used *Roman Glass* GP01-L, GP01-S, GP01-G, GP01-R, *Beads* GP04-L and GP04-S, *Artichokes* GP07-L and GP07-J, and *Forget-me-not Rose* GP08-L)

• **Binding fabric:** ½yd (46cm) of KAFFE FASSETT's *Exotic Stripe*-ES20 or a similar multi-coloured striped fabric
• **Quilting thread:** Mid rust-brown thread (machine-quilt the checkerboard with meandering squiggles, the striped baskets with parallel lines and the 'flowers' in the baskets with flower shapes)

pink flags

The diamond patches on the *Pink Flags* quilt are cut from many different types of print and a range of different colours. When selecting these, try to get a good balance of each colour and print type.

SIZE

The finished patchwork measures approximately 60in x 86¼in (152.5cm x 219cm).

Note that any measurements on the diagrams are for finished patch sizes, excluding the seam allowances.

Special cutting note: The pieced 'flags' on this quilt are stitched together using whole diamond patches and then trimmed to a triangle shape afterwards. This eliminates the need for cutting partial diamonds, and means you can change the diamonds around on your design wall until you get the colour sequences you like, without having to cut and recut partial triangles. If you take diamonds out of your blocks to replace them with other ones, you can just use these eliminated diamonds anywhere in another block.

INGREDIENTS

44–45in (112–114cm) wide 100% cotton fabrics:

• **Fabric A:** 3yd (2.8m) of KAFFE FASSETT'S 'pink' *Roman Glass* (GP01-PK) or a similar medium-scale print with high pastel circles on a bright pink ground

• **Fabric B:** ¼–½yd (25–46cm) each of at least 20 different monochromatic and multi-coloured prints in broad and narrow stripes, Japanese florals, and small polka dots, plus some two-toned stripes and small checks – all in a high palette of bright lime, sky blues, yellows, dusty pinks, orange-reds, greys and deep mustard (we included scraps

of KAFFE FASSETT's *Pressed Roses* PR06 and PR02 in this fabric group)

• **Backing fabric:** 4yd (3.7m)

• **Binding fabric:** ¾yd (70cm) of a crisp, bright-coloured stripe

• **Lightweight cotton batting:** 67in x 94in (170cm x 237cm)

• **Quilting thread:** Pale aqua thread

• **Templates:** Use template L on page 156, and make your own templates for the large triangles as explained

MAKING LARGE TRIANGLE TEMPLATES

The templates needed for the large pink triangles are too big to include in this book, so you'll need to make your own. Following the diagram for the measurements, draw the whole triangle (template J) and the two half triangles (templates K and reverse K) on a large sheet of sewing pattern paper. Then add the same seam allowance all

TEMPLATE

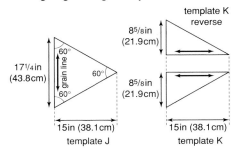

template L

Making large triangle templates

template K
reverse

8⅝in
(21.9cm)

17¼in
(43.8cm)

60°

60°

60°

8⅝in
(21.9cm)

15in (38.1cm)

template J

15in (38.1cm)

template K

around the shapes as on the diamond template (template L on page 156). Use the paper templates to cut your patches, or glue them to stiff cardboard if you want to trace around them.

CUTTING PATCHES

18 large triangles: Cut 18 template-J triangles from fabric A.

4 large half-triangles: Cut two template-K triangles and two template-K reverse triangles from fabric A.

18 flag blocks: For each of the 18 flag blocks, cut a total of 15 template-L diamonds, cutting five from one fabric B, four from another fabric B, three from another fabric B, two from another fabric B and one from another fabric B. (**Note:** There are two grain lines on template L. If possible, it is best to alternate the position of the grain line from row to row, so that the grain line of the first row of patches faces in one direction and the grain line on the next row of patches faces in the other direction. This is so that a bias edge is always stitched to an edge cut on the straight grain.)

4 half-flag blocks: For each of the 4 half-flag blocks, cut a total of nine template-L diamonds, cutting three from one fabric B, two from another fabric B, two from another fabric B,

Trimming pieced blocks

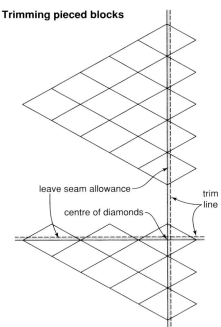

leave seam allowance

centre of diamonds

trim line

one from another fabric B and one from another fabric B.

MAKING BLOCKS

18 flag blocks: Make 18 flag blocks, joining the 15 diamonds cut for each block as shown in the diagram. (Use the seam allowance marked on the templates throughout.)

4 half-flag blocks: Make two half-flag blocks, joining the nine diamonds cut for each block as shown in the diagram. Then make two more half-flags in the same way, but joining them to make a 'reverse' shape.

TRIMMING BLOCKS

Press the pieced flag blocks and half-flag blocks. Then following the diagram, trim the blocks leaving a seam allowance along the trimmed edges.

ASSEMBLING PATCHWORK

Following the assembly diagram, arrange the flag blocks and large pink triangles on the floor or on a cotton-flannel design wall (see page 144). Once you have achieved the desired effect, sew the flag blocks and pink triangles together in rows, then join the rows.

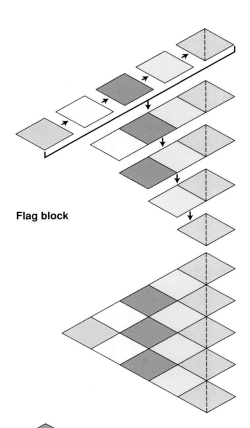

Flag block

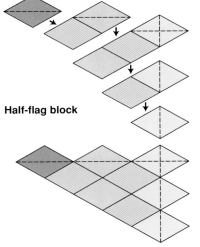

Half-flag block

FINISHING

Press the quilt top. Then without stretching the edges, run a long, straight, machine basting stitch around the outside edge of the quilt. This machine basting will help stabilize the bias edges on the diamonds while the patchwork is quilted.

Layer the quilt top, batting and backing; and baste (see page 148). Using pale aqua thread, machine-quilt parallel lines (parallel to the long edges of the

ASSEMBLY

quilt) spaced apart so that they run through the centres of the diamonds. Trim the quilt edges. Then cut the

striped binding fabric on the bias and attach (see page 149). Remove any visible basting thread.

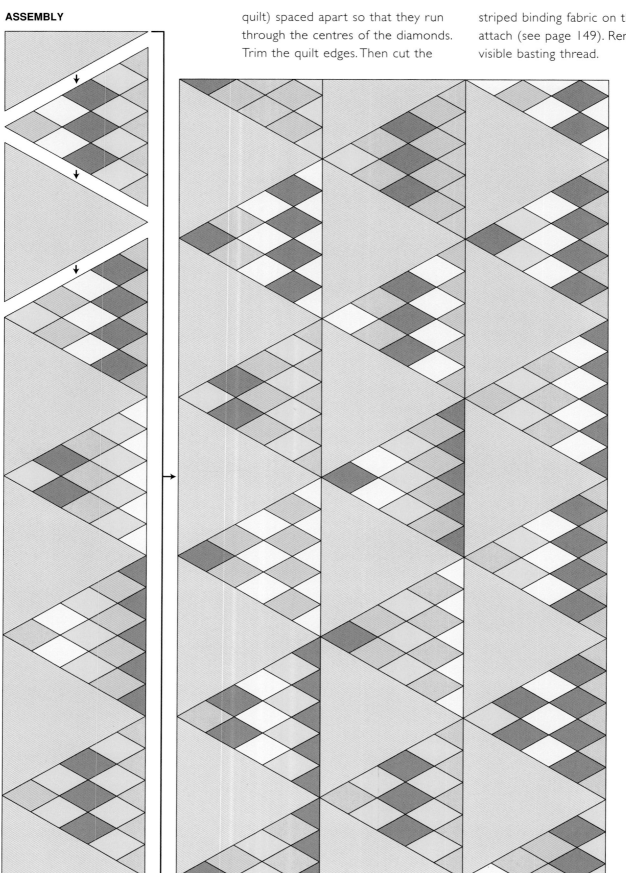

Key

fabric A

fabric B

pinwheel tablecloth

If you are trying to simulate the feel of this patchwork don't choose screaming colours. Although the colours look bright, they are actually faded jewel tones. Some scraps of all KAFFE FASSETT's *Pressed Roses* prints were used in this quilt, so if you have any scraps of these yourself, you might like to add them in.

SIZE

The finished patchwork measures approximately 50in × 50in (127cm × 127cm).
Note that any measurements on the diagrams are for finished patch sizes, excluding the seam allowances.

Special note: This patchwork is not quilted, but is instead 'fused' to the backing fabric with fusible web, which comes backed with paper and in various weights. A medium-heavy weight is suitable for this tablecloth.

INGREDIENTS

44–45in (112–114cm) wide 100% cotton fabrics in mostly solid colours and monochromatic prints that appear solid, plus some prints with dots and squares:
• **Fabric A:** ¼yd (25cm) each of at least five different fabrics in medium to dark tones of reds, rusts,

terracottas and hot pinks
• **Fabric B:** ¼yd (25cm) each of at least five different fabrics in medium to dark tones of teals, denim blues, gentian blues, pine greens and purples
• **Fabric C:** ¼yd (25cm) each of at least five different fabrics in light to medium tones of pinks, oranges and gold
• **Fabric D:** ¼yd (25cm) each of at least five different fabrics in light to medium tones of lavenders, limes, pale blues, duck-egg blue and apple greens
• **Fusible web:** Enough fusible web to cover the entire patchwork (see Special note)

• **Backing fabric:** 1¾yd of a 60in (152cm) wide cotton fabric that is slightly heavier than normal quilt fabric
• **Binding:** 7yd (6.5m) of 1in (2.5cm) wide deep wine grosgrain ribbon
• **Templates:** Use templates S and T on pages 150 and 152

CUTTING PATCHES

When cutting the triangles, cut about an equal number of matched sets from each of the four fabric groups.
136 large triangles: Cut 34 matching sets of four template-S triangles, for a total of 136 triangles.

TEMPLATES

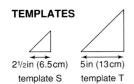

2½in (6.5cm)
template S

5in (13cm)
template T

Large pinwheel

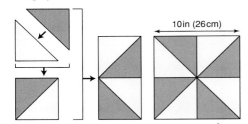

10in (26cm)

Small pinwheel

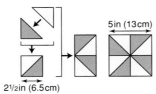

5in (13cm)

2½in (6.5cm)

Small pinwheel block

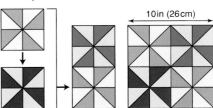

10in (26cm)

pinwheel tablecloth

ASSEMBLY

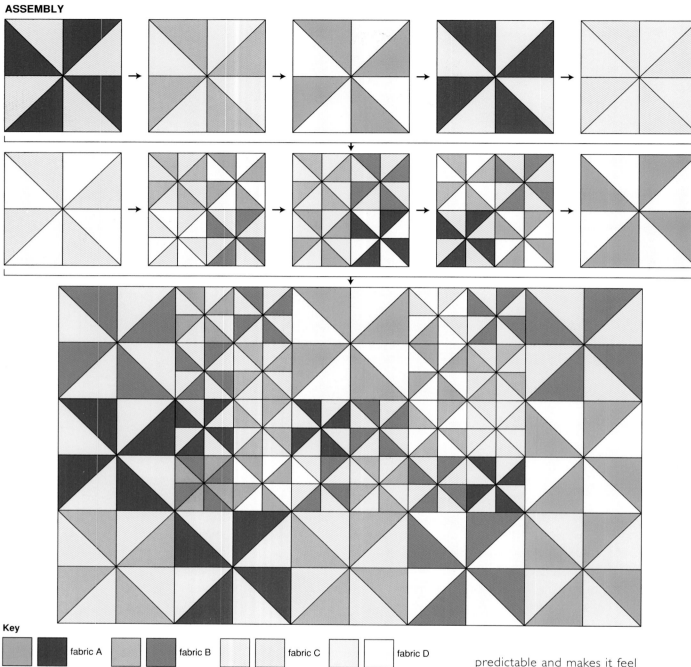

Key

fabric A fabric B fabric C fabric D

256 small triangles: Cut 64 matching sets of four template-T triangles, for a total of 256 triangles.

MAKING PINWHEELS

Most of the pinwheels are made by combining four matching triangles in a darker shade (fabric A or B) with four matching triangles in a lighter shade (fabric C or D). Fabric A is usually paired with fabric D, and fabric B with

fabric C. Many of the pinwheels are made from two colours that are complementary so that blues are paired with yellow/orange tones, and reds with green/blue-green tones – this is only a guideline to help with the selection of the colour pairs. Also, a few of the pinwheels were made with a 'mistake' fabric so that one of the blades is different from the other three; this helps keep the pattern less

predictable and makes it feel whimsical.

The positions of the darker triangles are what make the pinwheels 'spin' in one direction or the other. Don't make all the pinwheels spin in the same direction.

17 large pinwheels: Make 17 large pinwheels, joining four matching large triangles to four other matching large triangles as shown in the diagram. (Use the seam allowance marked on the templates throughout.)

32 small pinwheels: Make 32 small pinwheels, joining four matching small triangles to four other matching small triangles as shown in the diagram.

ARRANGING PINWHEELS

Following the assembly diagram, arrange all the pinwheels in the desired quilt arrangement before making the small pinwheel blocks. You can make the arrangement on the floor or on a design wall (see page 144).

MAKING SMALL PINWHEEL BLOCKS

8 small pinwheel blocks: Once you have achieved the desired effect with the arrangement, make eight small pinwheel blocks, joining groups of four small pinwheels together as shown in the diagram.

ASSEMBLING PATCHWORK

Sew the large pinwheels and the small pinwheel blocks together in rows, then join the rows.

FINISHING

Press the patchwork very well. If necessary, trim the edges to straighten them, but do not cut off the seam allowance. Then carefully press the fusible web to the wrong side of the patchwork. (Be sure to follow the manufacturer's instructions for ironing on the fusible web.)

Next, press the backing fabric. Peel the paper-backing off the fusible web and place the backing fabric on top of the exposed web. Press the whole sandwich very slowly to fuse the layers firmly together.

Trim the excess backing fabric around the edges. Fold the grosgrain ribbon over the seam allowance around the edge of the patchwork, pinning and then basting in place. Machine topstitch the ribbon, and remove the basting.

ginger jars

The jars on this quilt are cut from a KAFFE FASSETT print called *Pressed Roses* (see page 159 for fabric information). To achieve the same effect with your own collection of scraps, aim for an overall mood of pink and red.

SIZE

The finished patchwork measures approximately 79in × 101in (200.5cm × 256.5cm).

Note that measurements on the diagrams are for finished patch sizes, excluding the seam allowances.

Special note: Each horizontal row of 11 triangles can be cut from a piece of fabric about 3½in (9cm) by 44in (112cm), so it is best not to buy 'fat quarters' (which are too narrow) for this project.

INGREDIENTS

44–45in (112–114cm) wide 100% cotton fabrics:
• **Fabric A ('red' zigzags):** ¼–½yd (25–46cm) each of at least 10 different monochromatic small-scale prints in dark-toned magentas, wines and scarlet, plus KAFFE FASSETT'S *Narrow Stripe*-NS17 or a similar narrow,

TEMPLATES

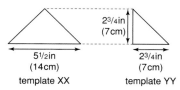

2¾in
(7cm)

5½in
(14cm)

2¾in
(7cm)

template XX

template YY

Ginger-jar template

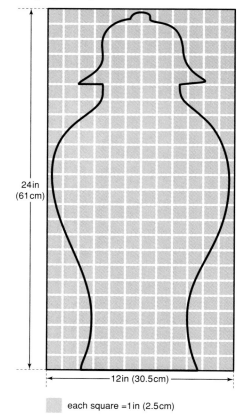

24in
(61cm)

12in (30.5cm)

each square = 1in (2.5cm)

Quilting for Ginger Jars

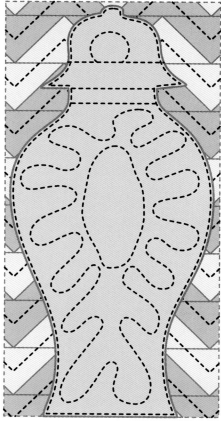

multi-coloured stripe in mostly dark magentas and reds
• **Fabric B ('pink' zigzags):** ¼–½yd (25–46cm) each of at least 10 different monochromatic small-scale prints, plaids and one stripe in fresh pinks, dusty pinks and grey-pinks
• **Fabric C (border 1):** ½yd (46cm) of an almost solid-looking monochromatic print in deep magenta
• **Fabric D (border 1):** ½yd (46cm) of KAFFE FASSETT's 'grass' *Shot Cotton* (SC27) or a similar solid-coloured deep aqua fabric
• **Fabric E (border 2):** ½yd (46cm) of an almost solid-looking monochromatic print in vivid moss green
• **Fabric F (border 3):** 2½yd (2.3m) of KAFFE FASSETT's *Pressed Roses*-PR04 or a similar bicolour print with light salmon flowers on a deep plum ground
• **Fabric G (ginger jars):** 3½yd (3.2m) of KAFFE FASSETT's *Pressed Roses*-PR06 or a similar bicolour print with cream flowers on a coral red ground
• **Lightweight interfacing:** Enough to back 15 jars, each approximately 12in × 24½in (30.5cm × 62.5cm)
• **Backing fabric:** 6yd (5.5m)
• **Binding fabric:** 1yd (91cm) of KAFFE FASSETT's *Narrow Stripe*-NS09 or a similar narrow, dark plummy multi-coloured stripe
• **Lightweight cotton batting:** 86in × 108in (219cm × 275cm)
• **Quilting thread:** Dark magenta thread
• **Templates and appliqués:** Use templates XX and YY on page 152, and make your own jar appliqué template as instructed

CUTTING PATCHES
Quilt centre
15 'red' zigzags: For each of the 15 'red' horizontal zigzags, cut 21 template-XX triangles and two template-YY triangles from a single fabric A.

14 'pink' zigzags: For each of the 14 'pink' horizontal zigzags, cut 21 template-XX triangles and two template-YY triangles from a single fabric B.

2 'pink' half-zigzags: For the 'pink' half-zigzag at the *top* of the quilt centre, cut 11 template-XX triangles from a single fabric B. For the 'pink' half-zigzag at the *bottom* of the quilt centre, cut 10 template-XX triangles and two template-YY triangles from a single fabric B.

Border 1
Fabric-C (deep magenta) triangles: Cut 51 template-XX triangles and six template-YY triangles from fabric C.

Fabric-D (deep aqua) triangles: Cut 53 template-XX triangles and two template-YY triangles from fabric D.

Border 2
4 strips: From fabric E, cut two strips 2in × 66½in (5cm × 169cm) and two strips 2in × 91½in (5cm × 232.5cm).

Border 3
4 strips: From fabric F, cut two strips 5½in × 69½in (14cm × 176.5cm) and two strips 5½in × 101½in (14cm × 258cm).

PREPARING JAR APPLIQUÉS
Following the diagram, draw the ginger jar shape on a large piece of graph paper or sewing pattern paper. Cut the shape out. (If you want a stiff template, glue the shape to a piece of cardboard and cut out.) Trace 15 jars on the wrong side of the jar fabric (fabric G), leaving a gap between the

ASSEMBLY

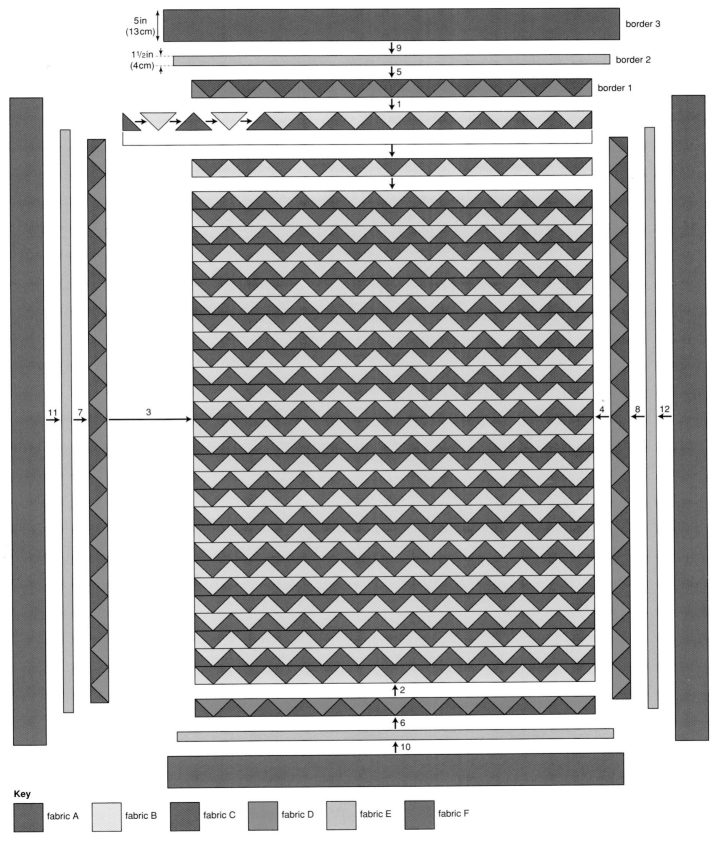

5in (13cm)

1½in (4cm)

border 3

border 2

border 1

Key
fabric A   fabric B   fabric C   fabric D   fabric E   fabric F

shapes for ¼in (6mm) seam allowances. Cut out the jars ¼in (6mm) outside the outline. Cut 15 jars the same size (including the seam allowance) from the lightweight interfacing.

With right sides together, sew each fabric jar to an interfacing jar, stitching along the traced outline all around the shape. Clip and notch the seam allowance along the curves and at the corners as necessary. Then slit a hole in the centre of the interfacing, big enough for turning the jar right side out. Turn right side out and press the finished jars, pressing the seam line slightly towards the wrong side. Set the appliqués aside until the patchwork is complete.

ASSEMBLING PATCHWORK
Quilt centre
Following the assembly diagram, arrange the triangles in 30 rows of zigzag stripes, starting a 'red' zigzag at the top and alternating 'red' and 'pink' zigzags. Then arrange the 'pink' half-zigzags at the top and bottom.

Make the arrangement on the floor or on a cotton-flannel design wall (see page 144).

Once you have achieved the desired effect, sew the patches together in rows, then join the rows as shown. (Use the seam allowance marked on the templates throughout.)

Border 1
For the top border, join together 11 template-XX fabric-C triangles, and 10 template-XX and two template-YY fabric-D triangles as shown. Sew to the top of the quilt centre.

For the bottom border, join together 11 template-XX fabric-D triangles, and 10 template-XX and two template-YY fabric-C triangles as shown. Sew to the bottom of the quilt centre.

For each of the two side borders, join

together 16 template-XX fabric-D triangles, and 15 template-XX and two template-YY fabric-C triangles as shown. Sew to the quilt centre.

Borders 2 and 3
Sew the short fabric-E strips to the top and bottom of the quilt, and then the long fabric-E strips to the sides. Next, sew on the fabric-F strips in the same way.

GINGER JAR APPLIQUÉ
Press the assembled patchwork. Then baste three rows of five prepared jars to the patchwork, spacing the three rows evenly apart between the top and bottom of the quilt centre and spacing the five jars in each row evenly apart with the outer jars just touching the vivid moss green border 2. Topstitch the jars in place close to the edge using the dark magenta quilting thread.

Cut away the background fabric and interfacing behind each ginger jar to within about ¼in (6mm) of the topstitching.

FINISHING
Press the quilt top. Layer the quilt top, batting and backing; and baste (see page 148).

Using a dark magenta thread, machine-quilt a zigzag along the middle of each zigzag in the quilt centre. Outline quilt ¾in (2cm) from the triangle point of each fabric-C (deep magenta) triangle in border 1. Machine-quilt the jars following the diagram – do this free-form, as the quilting on the jars doesn't have to match exactly.

On border 3, machine-quilt a single large, free-form zigzag along each of the strips.

Trim the quilt edges. Then cut the striped binding fabric on the bias and attach (see page 149).

handkerchief corners

Handerkerchief Corners is made from KAFFE FASSETT's multi-coloured stripe fabrics and some solids (see page 127). All the colourways of the various stripes are included except for the palest ones. If you want to use other stripe fabrics but achieve the same colour effect, stick to smoldering, earthy autumnal colours with accents of jewel magentas, turquoises, lavenders and blues.

SIZE
The finished patchwork measures approximately 78in x 78in (198cm x 198cm).

Note that measurements on the diagrams are for finished patch sizes, excluding the seam allowances – except for diagrams showing how to cut patches from joined strips.

INGREDIENTS
45in (114cm) wide 100% cotton KAFFE FASSETT *quilt fabrics:*
• **Fabric A (stripes):** ¼yd (25cm) each of at least 25 different *Stripes* (*Pachrangi, Alternate, Narrow, Broad* and *Exotic*) or 25 similar multi-coloured medium- and large-scale woven striped fabrics (see above for colour theme) – alternatively, buy ½yd (46cm) of at least 12 different stripes
• **Fabric B (solids):** ¼yd (25cm) each of *Shot Cotton* in 'chartreuse' (SC12), 'mustard' (SC16) and 'tobacco' (SC18), or three similar solid-coloured fabrics in deep chartreuse, mustard and tobacco brown

TEMPLATES

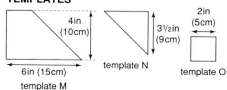

4in (10cm)
6in (15cm)
template M

3½in (9cm)
template N

2in (5cm)
template O

Cutting patches from joined strips

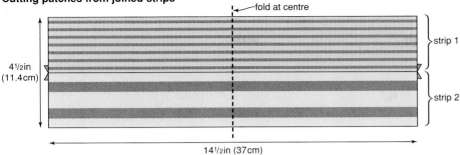

fold at centre

strip 1

strip 2

4½in (11.4cm)

14½in (37cm)

- **Backing fabric:** 5yd (4.6m)
- **Binding fabric:** ¾yd (70cm) extra of a fabric A for bias binding
- **Lightweight cotton batting:** 85in × 85in (216cm × 216cm)
- **Quilting thread:** Medium-toned, neutral-coloured thread
- **Templates:** Use templates M, N and O on page 153

CUTTING PATCHES

120 template-O squares: From fabric B (solids), cut a total of 120 template-O squares for the 120 large blocks.

120 large blocks and 144 small blocks: The rest of the patches for the blocks are cut from joined strips of different striped fabrics. First, cut *240 strips* 2½in × 14½in (6.4cm × 37cm) from fabric A, with the stripes running lengthways. Then, cut *24 strips* 2½in × 9½in (6.4cm × 24cm) from fabric A, again with the stripes running lengthways.

Join two different fabric-A 14½in (37cm) strips together along the long edges, using the seam allowance marked on the templates. Open out the strips and press. Join all the remaining 14½in (37cm) strips together in the same way to make a

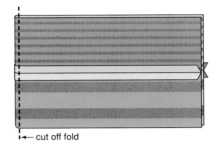

cut off fold

template N

template M

first cut
second cut

total of **120 long joined strips**. Then join the 9½in (24cm) strips in the same way to make a total of **12 short joined strips**.

Follow the cutting diagram when cutting the template-M and template-N patches. First, fold a 14½in (37cm) joined strip in half widthways with the right side of the fabric together. Then using a rotary cutter and mat (see page 144), cut off the fold about ⅛in (3mm) from the crease and discard.

So that the two layers remain perfectly aligned, DO NOT separate or move them. Keeping the two layers of fabric together, cut the template-M trapezoid patches and the template-N triangle patches placing the templates on the fabric in the exact positions shown on the template illustrations on page 153. To do this, first cut the 45° diagonal, then trim the template-N patches along the right edge. Since they will have to be stitched together in this position to make the blocks, keep the matching triangle patches right sides together and the matching trapezoid patches right sides together. Cut a total of 120 matching pairs of template-M trapezoids and 120 matching pairs of template-N triangles in this way from the 14½in (37cm) joined strips.

Cut the remaining 24 matching pairs of template-N triangles from the 9½in (24cm) joined strips. Use the same method as before, folding the strips in half, then cutting matched patches – but cut two pairs of matching template-N triangles from each folded strip.

QUILT CENTRE
Making blocks
144 small blocks: Make 144 small blocks, joining each pair of matching

Large block

Cut from joined strips

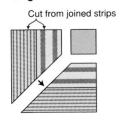

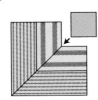

6in (15cm)

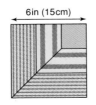

Small block

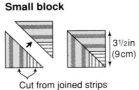

3½in (9cm)

Cut from joined strips

ASSEMBLY

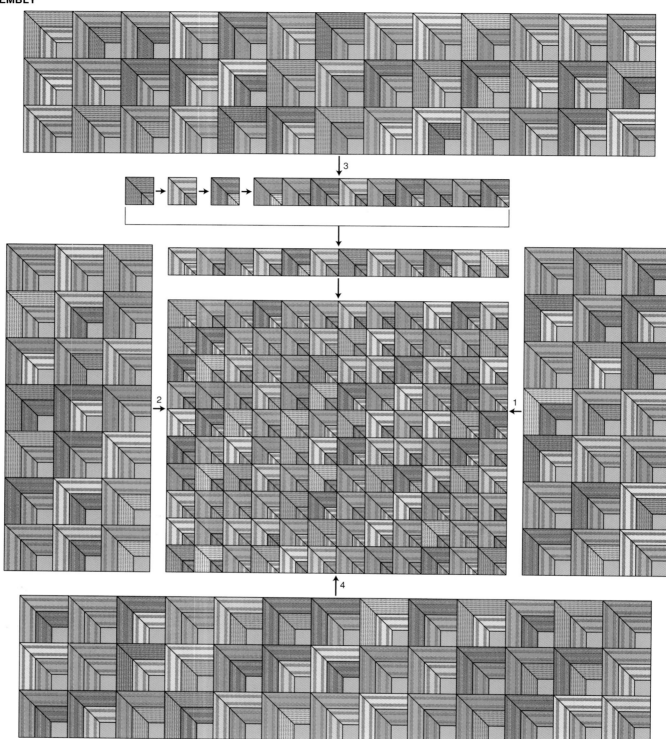

template-N triangles along the diagonal as shown in the diagram. (Use the seam allowance marked on the templates throughout.)

Assembling quilt centre

Following the assembly diagram, arrange the small blocks in 12 rows of 12 blocks, with the blocks all facing in the same direction. Make the arrangement on the floor or on a cotton-flannel design wall (see page 144). Once you have achieved the desired effect, sew the blocks together in rows, then join the rows.

BORDER

Making blocks

120 large blocks: Make 120 large blocks, joining each pair of matching template-M trapezoids along the diagonal as shown in the diagram, then stitching on a template-O square with

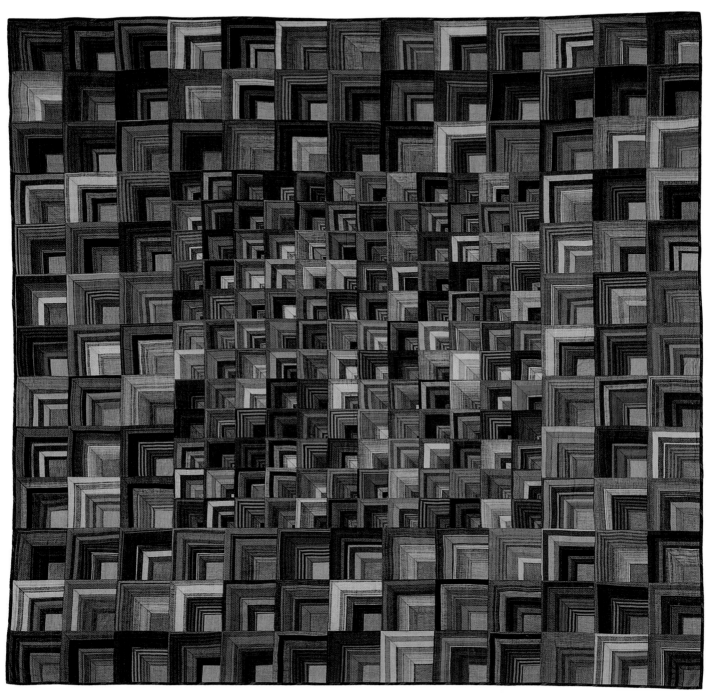

an inset seam (see page 147).

Assembling border

Following the assembly diagram, arrange a border three large blocks deep all around the quilt centre, with the blocks all facing in the same direction.

Once you have achieved the desired effect, stitch together the blocks for each of the two side borders by joining the blocks into long rows, then joining the rows. Sew the assembled side borders to the quilt centre. Stitch together the blocks for the top and bottom borders in the same way, then sew them to the quilt centre.

FINISHING

Press the quilt top. Layer the quilt top, batting and backing; and baste (see page 148 for how to do this).

Using a medium-toned, neutral-coloured thread, machine-quilt in-the-ditch on all the patch seams on the large blocks. Quilt in-the-ditch around the outside of the small blocks and on the diagonal seams.

Trim the quilt edges. Then cut the striped binding fabric on the bias and attach (see page 149).

optical squares tablecloth

The *Optical Squares Tablecloth* is made entirely from leftover scraps of KAFFE FASSETT multi-coloured Indian stripe fabrics (see page 159 for information about the KAFFE FASSETT Fabric Collection). The resulting quilt has an overall look of red/maroon with ochre notes (see page 61).

If you are trying to approximate the look of our version with your own selection of stripes, keep the tones medium to dark.

Special note: If you are collecting scraps of striped fabrics for this quilt, be sure to take into consideration that the stripes run parallel to the longest side of each triangle patch – so each scrap needs to be a minimum of 10½in × 6in (27cm × 15.5cm).

SIZE

The finished patchwork measures approximately 54in × 54in (137cm × 137cm).
Note that any measurements on the diagrams are for finished patch sizes, excluding the seam allowances.

INGREDIENTS

45in (114cm) wide 100% cotton KAFFE FASSETT quilt fabrics:

• **Patch fabrics:** Assorted scraps or ¼–½yd (25–46cm) each of at least 8–10 different *Stripes* (*Pachrangi, Alternate, Narrow, Broad* and *Exotic*), or 8–10 similar multi-coloured medium- and large-scale woven stripe fabrics,

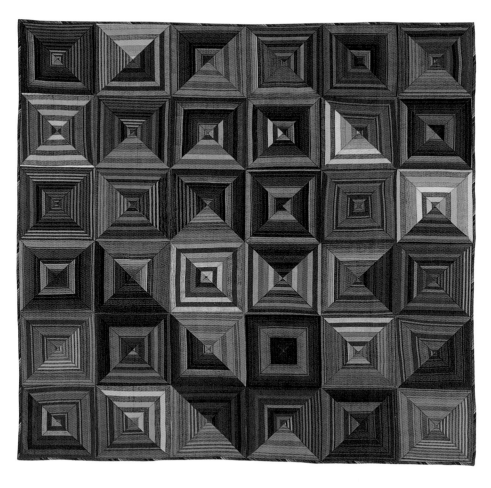

predominantly in medium to dark tones of purples, plums, oranges and reds, plus some greens and blues
• **Backing fabric:** 3½yd (3.2m) – buy more if making a larger size
• **Binding fabric:** ½yd (46cm) extra of one of striped patch fabrics for bias binding
• **Lightweight cotton batting:** 61in × 61in (155cm × 155cm)
• **Quilting thread:** Grey-green thread
• **Template:** Use template V on page 156

CUTTING PATCHES

144 triangles: Cut 144 template-V triangles from the assorted striped fabrics, making sure that the stripes run parallel to the longest side of the template. (The stripes aren't meant to line up when sewn together, so don't worry about this when cutting your striped patches.)

MAKING BLOCKS

36 mitred blocks: Make 36 mitred blocks, joining four template-V

TEMPLATE

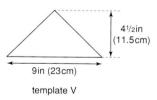

4½in (11.5cm)

9in (23cm)

template V

Mitred block

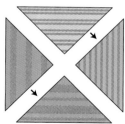 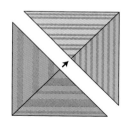 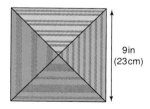

9in (23cm)

ASSEMBLY

triangles for each block as shown in the diagram. Make some of the blocks with four different stripes, some with three different stripes, some with two different stripes, and two or three blocks with just one stripe. (Use the seam allowance marked on the template throughout.)

ASSEMBLING PATCHWORK

Arrange the blocks in six rows of six blocks, either on the floor or on a cotton-flannel design wall. (See page 144 for how to make your own self-standing design wall from two large boards covered with cotton flannel, which the patches will stick to.) Once you have achieved the desired effect, sew the blocks together in rows, then join the rows.

FINISHING

Press the quilt top carefully. Then layer the quilt top, batting and backing; and baste them together (see page 148 for how to do this).

Using grey-green thread (or another neutral colour that will not show up), machine-quilt horizontal, vertical and diagonal lines in-the-ditch between the patches.

Trim the quilt edges. Then cut the striped binding fabric on the bias and attach (see page 149 for how to attach a binding around the edge of your patchwork).

shirt-stripe boxes

Four identical striped patches are pieced together to form each mitred block on this quilt, and the lined-up stripes create concentric squares on the block. Don't go crazy trying to match the stripe seams perfectly though. Let them wiggle a little – this is supposed to be fun!

SIZE

The finished patchwork measures approximately 54in × 87in (137cm × 221cm).
Note that any measurements on the diagrams are for finished patch sizes, excluding the seam allowances.

Special note: At first glance, the individual blocks in this quilt might appear to be made entirely of matching fabric stripes that form blocks with exact concentric squares. But many of the blocks have mismatched fabrics, and some have mismatched stripes. The blocks are cut in sets of four identical triangle patches, then some of the triangles are mixed together.

TEMPLATES

9in (23cm) 6in (15cm) 3in (7.5cm)
template V template W template X

INGREDIENTS

44–60in (112–153cm) wide 100% cotton shirting fabrics:
• **Patch fabrics:** ¼–½yd (25–46cm) each of at least 15 different woven striped shirting fabrics, predominantly in blue-and-white stripes, and red, blue, and white stripes – we added in a few scraps of KAFFE FASSETT's blue *Ombré Stripe* (OS02) and narrow *Blue-and-White Stripe* (BWS01)
• **Backing fabric:** 5½yd (5m)

• **Binding fabric:** ¾yd (70cm) extra of one of the blue-and-white patch stripes
• **Lightweight cotton batting:** 61in × 94in (155cm × 239cm)
• **Quilting thread:** Pale blue thread
• **Template:** Use templates V, W and X on pages 153 and 156

CUTTING PATCHES

20 large mitred blocks: From the assorted striped fabrics, cut 20 sets of four matching template-V triangles. Cut each set so that the stripes run parallel to the longest side of the template and so that the four fabric

ASSEMBLY

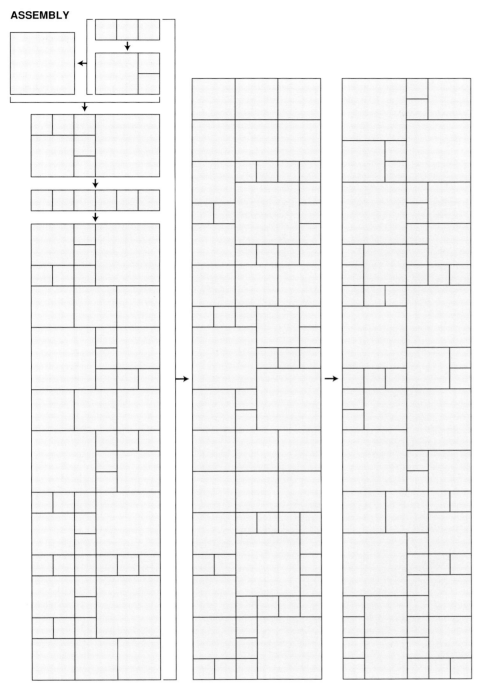

Mitred blocks

9in (23cm)
large mitred block

6in (15cm)
medium-size
mitred block

3in (7.5cm)
small
mitred
block

Also, take a few patch sets with the same fabrics and mix these so that the fabrics will match in the block but the stripes won't.

20 large mitred blocks: Make 20 large mitred blocks, joining a set of four template-V triangles for each block as shown in the block diagram for the *Optical Squares Tablecloth* on page 128. (Use the seam allowance marked on the templates throughout.)

53 medium-size mitred blocks: Make 53 medium-size mitred blocks, joining a set of four template-W triangles for each block.

130 small mitred blocks: Make 130 small mitred blocks, joining a set of four template-X triangles for each block.

ASSEMBLING PATCHWORK

Following the assembly diagram and keeping the darkest blocks well scattered, arrange the blocks in three long strips, either on the floor or on a cotton-flannel design wall (see page 144). Once you have achieved the desired effect, join the blocks in each strip, piecing them together carefully so that there is never any need for inset seams. Then join the three strips.

FINISHING

Press the quilt top. Layer the quilt top, batting and backing; and baste (see page 148).

Using pale blue thread, machine-quilt in-the-ditch only on the diagonal patch seams. Trim the quilt edges. Then cut the striped binding fabric on the bias and attach (see page 149).

triangles are identical.

53 medium-size mitred blocks: From the assorted striped fabrics, cut 53 sets of four matching template-W triangles as explained for the large mitred blocks.

130 small mitred blocks: From the assorted striped fabrics, cut 130 sets of four matching template-X triangles as explained above for the large mitred blocks.

MAKING MITRED BLOCKS

Before making the mitred blocks, mix some of the patch sets together so that some of the blocks will have mismatched fabrics with two or three different fabrics in a block. Do this randomly so that there will be about two large blocks, about four medium-size blocks and about 16 small blocks with mismatched fabrics.

stars and stripes

This striking patchwork with its fresh and sassy blue-and-white stars is not for faint-hearted stitchers – there is lots of advanced piecing with inset seams (see page 147 for tips). The wonderful results, however, will be worth all the effort.

SIZE

The finished patchwork quilt measures approximately 91in × 94in (230cm × 239cm). (The quilting stitches will slightly draw in the final measurements of the patchwork.)

Note that any measurements on the diagrams are for finished patch sizes, excluding the seam allowances.

INGREDIENTS

44–45in (112–114cm) wide 100% cotton fabrics:

• **Fabric A (blue centre stars):** ½yd (46cm) of at least 15 different blue-and-white or blue-and-off-white fabrics, predominantly in narrow and bold stripes, large-scale ginghams and plaids, plus some small-scale prints

TEMPLATES

9in
(23cm)

4¹/₂in
(11.5cm)

9in
(23cm)

4¹/₂in
(11.5cm)

template M   template N   template O   template P
                                              and P reverse

Star blocks

4¹/₂in (11.5cm)

ASSEMBLY

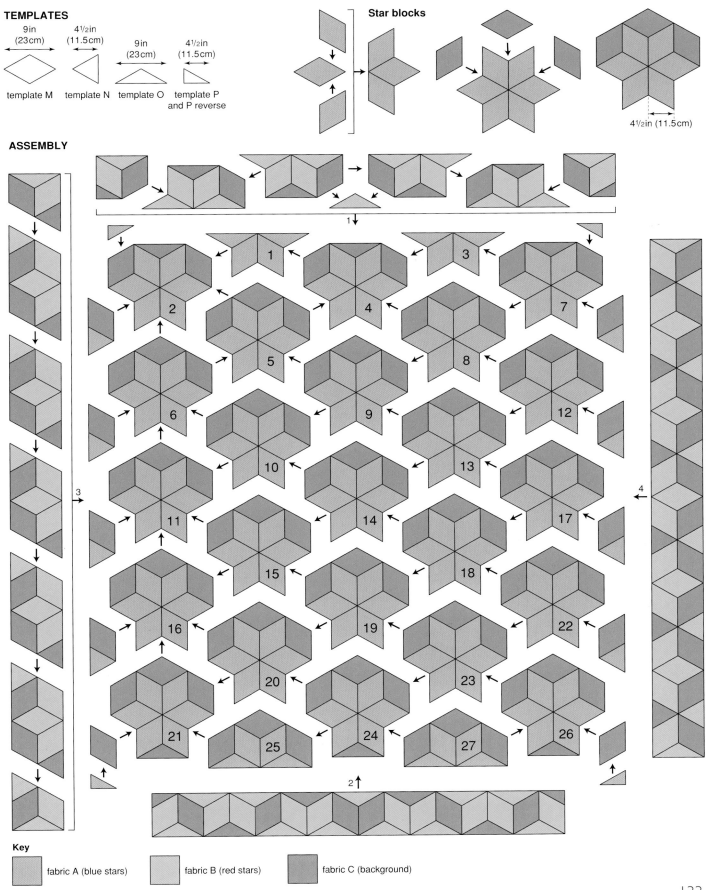

Key

fabric A (blue stars)   fabric B (red stars)   fabric C (background)

133

Quilting for Stars and Stripes

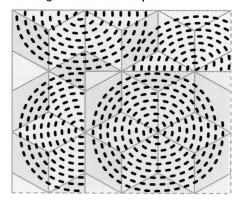

- **Fabric B (red border stars):** ½yd (46cm) of at least six different burgundy-and-white or burgundy-and-cream fabrics in bold stripes and prints
- **Fabric C (background):** 3yd (2.8m) of a single large-scale floral print in beige, pinks and red on a grease-brown ground (see binding fabric)
- **Backing fabric:** 7yd (5.3m)
- **Binding fabric:** 1yd (91cm) extra of fabric C
- **Cotton batting:** 98in × 101in (248cm × 257cm)
- **Quilting thread:** Thick cotton embroidery thread and/or lightweight cotton knitting yarns in bright and dark reds, mauve and coral for quilt centre, and blues for border
- **Templates:** Use templates M, N, O, P and P reverse on page 151

CUTTING PATCHES

Pay attention to the direction of the stripes on the fabrics when you are cutting the patches.

Quilt centre

23 stars: For each of the 23 full stars, cut a set of six template-M diamonds, cutting about half of the total number of sets each from a single fabric A and about half of the sets each from two A fabrics.

4 half-stars: For each of the four half-stars, cut a matching set of two template-M diamonds and two template-O half-diamonds from a single fabric A.

8 star points: For the individual points along the sides of the quilt centre, cut eight template-N triangles from different A fabrics.

4 corner triangles: For the small corner triangles on the quilt centre, cut four triangles (two using template P and two using P reverse) from different A fabrics.

Quilt centre background: From fabric C, cut 82 template-M diamonds and six template-O half-diamonds.

Border

12 half-stars: For each of the 12 half-stars, cut a matching set of two template-M diamonds and two template-O half-diamonds from a single fabric B.

10 three-pointed half-stars: For each of the 10 three-pointed half-stars, cut a matching set of three template-M diamonds from a single fabric B.

Border background: From fabric C, cut 36 template-M diamonds, eight template-O half-diamonds, 12 template-N triangles, and four small corner triangles (two using template P and two using P reverse).

QUILT CENTRE

Making blocks

23 star blocks: Make 23 star blocks, joining one of the fabric-A sets of six diamonds and three fabric-C background diamonds for each block as shown in the diagram on page 133. (Use the seam allowance marked on the templates throughout, and see the basic patchwork techniques on page 147 for tips on how to stitch inset seams.)

4 half-star blocks: Make four half-star blocks, joining one of the matching fabric-A sets of two diamonds and two half-diamonds for each block; then join three fabric-A background

diamonds each to two of these blocks (see the assembly diagram shown on page 133).

8 small edging blocks: Make eight small edging blocks, joining one fabric-A star point (template N) and one fabric-C background diamond for each block.

Assembling quilt centre

Following the assembly diagram, arrange the blocks for the quilt centre on the floor or on a cotton-flannel design wall (see page 144).

Once you have achieved the desired effect, sew the blocks together in the sequence indicated, attaching block 1 to block 2; block 2 to the adjacent edging block; block 3 to block 4; block 4 to 1; block 5 to 4, 1 and 2; block 6 to 5, 2 and the adjacent edging blocks; and so on.

When all the blocks have been joined, add the four corner patches.

ASSEMBLING BORDER

Following the assembly diagram, join blocks for the four border strips. Attach the top and bottom border to the quilt centre first, then join on the side borders.

FINISHING

Press the quilt top. Layer the quilt top, batting and backing; and baste (see page 148).

Hand quilt each star freehand with concentric circles that spiral out from the centre as shown in the diagram above left, using bright and dark reds, mauve and coral for the blue stars, and blues for the red stars in the border strips.

Trim the quilt edges. Then cut the binding strips and attach (see page 149). If you use a stripe instead of a print for your binding, be sure to cut the strips on the bias for a more striking effect.

bright optical squares cushion

The instructions that follow are for the *Bright Optical Squares Cushion*. Descriptions of fabrics for an alternative colourway for the cushion are given on page 136 and this alternative version is pictured on page 66.

SIZE

The finished cushion cover patchwork measures approximately 18in x 18in (46cm x 46cm).
Note that any measurements on the diagrams are for finished patch sizes, excluding the seam allowances.

INGREDIENTS

44–45in (112–114cm) wide 100% cotton fabrics:
• **Patch fabrics:** Assorted scraps or ⅛yd (12cm) each of at least 6–10

different small- and medium-scale printed and woven striped fabrics (mostly multi-coloured with a few bicoloured), predominantly in reds, greens and golds, plus some blues and oranges – if desired, add a maverick small-scale printed plaid to enliven the fabric mixture
• **Backing fabric:** ¾yd (70cm)
• **Trimming:** 2¼yd (2m) red bobble fringe
• **Cushion pad/insert:** 18in x 18in (46cm x 46cm)
• **Template:** Use template X on page 153

CUTTING PATCHES

144 triangles: Cut 144 template-X triangles from the assorted striped fabrics, making sure that the stripes run parallel to the longest side of the

template. (The stripes aren't meant to line up when sewn together, so don't worry about this when cutting your striped patches.)

MAKING BLOCKS

36 mitred blocks: Make 36 mitred blocks, joining four template-X triangles for each block as shown in the diagram for the *Optical Squares Tablecloth* on page 128. Make some of the blocks with four different stripes, some with three different stripes, some with two different stripes and some with just one stripe. (Use the seam allowance marked on the template throughout.)

ASSEMBLING PATCHWORK

Following the assembly diagram for the *Optical Squares Tablecloth* on page 129, arrange the blocks in six rows of six blocks, either on the floor or on a cotton-flannel design wall (see page 144). Once you have achieved the desired effect, sew the blocks together in rows, then join the rows.

FINISHING

Press the patchwork. Cut a piece of backing fabric to exactly the same size as the patchwork. Before joining the backing and patchwork, stitch the fringe to the right side of the patchwork so it will be caught in the seam. With right sides together, stitch the patchwork to the backing around three sides, leaving the fourth side open. Turn the cover right side out, insert the cushion pad/insert and join the opening.

TEMPLATE

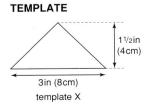

1½in (4cm)

3in (8cm)
template X

ALTERNATIVE COLOURWAY

Follow the instructions for the *Bright Optical Squares Cushion* to make the *Pastel Optical Squares Cushion*, but use the colours given here.

Pastel Optical Squares Cushion

• **Patch fabric:** Assorted scraps or ⅛yd (12cm) each of at least 6–10 different small- and medium-scale printed and woven striped fabrics (mostly bicoloured with a few multi-coloured), predominantly in chalky pastel dull rose pink stripes or pastel blue stripes on white or ecru grounds; plus a maverick multi-coloured striped fabric with bright yellow and blue-green to enliven the fabric mixture
• **Trimming:** 2¼yd (2m) grey-blue bobble fringe

turban footstool

This round patchwork with wedge-shaped patches can be made to fit any size round footstool. We chose a footstool manufactured for the needlepoint trade, measuring about 18in (46cm) in diameter (see page 158). Keep your fabric palette autumnal as explained in these instructions, or your choose own colour scheme.

INGREDIENTS

44–45in (112–114cm) wide 100% cotton fabrics:
• **Patch fabrics:** ¼yd (25cm) each of at least 16 medium- and small-scale spot prints in autumnal colours including rusty red, greeny golds, maroons, oranges and dark browns, plus two solid-coloured fabrics, one in lavender and one in teal – if desired use KAFFE FASSETT's 'lavender' and 'pine' (dark teal) *Shot Cotton* (SC14 and SC21) as the solid-coloured lavender and teal accents and include KAFFE FASSETT's 'jewel' *Beads* (GP04-J), 'jewel' *Pebble*

Beach (GP06-J), and *Exotic Stripe*-ES21 (mainly plums and reds) in your selection of prints like we did
• **Button fabric:** Scrap of KAFFE FASSETT's 'gold' *Roman Glass* (GP01-G) or a similar medium-scale circles print with a gold ground and jewel-coloured accents
• **Muslin:** 1yd (1m) of muslin
• **Button mould:** 2⅛in (5cm) button mould that will take a fabric covering
• **Round footstool**

CUTTING FOUNDATION PIECES

First measure the circumference of your footstool around the widest part (see the diagram on the next page), then divide this measurement by eight to determine the width of a one-eighth wedge of the stool (A). Next, measure the radius of the top (B). Lastly, measure from the edge of the radius to about 4in (10cm) under

the footstool, where the cover will be attached (C). Draw the shape and size of a one-eighth wedge of the footstool on a piece of paper – don't worry about tapering the shape back in under the footstool as this will be pleated in as the finished patchwork is attached.

Place your paper template on your footstool and check that it covers exactly one-eighth of the stool. It's better to be a little generous with the size rather than too skimpy. Adjust and recut if necessary.

Using the paper template, draw the shape on the muslin and cut out, leaving a ¾in (2cm) seam allowance along the two long sides. Trace and cut seven more foundation pieces in the same way.

On each foundation piece, draw the positions for eight strips of fabric, from roughly the top centre to the

Marking one eighth of footstool

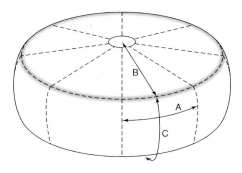

Foundation pieces

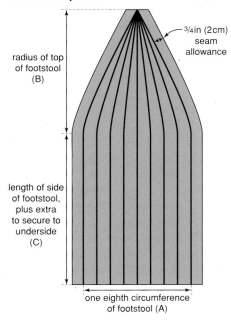

radius of top of footstool (B)

¾in (2cm) seam allowance

length of side of footstool, plus extra to secure to underside (C)

one eighth circumference of footstool (A)

bottom edge, fanning out from the centre. The strips should not be perfectly equal in width and the tops to not need to meet exactly in the middle. A big button will cover up quite a lot of the top 1in (2.5cm) of the wedges.

CUTTING STRIP PATCHES

Cut the assorted patch fabrics into strips approximately 2in (5cm) wide and a bit longer than your foundation pieces – it is best to cut a few strips from each of your fabrics to start with and then cut more as you use them up on your patch wedges.

MAKING PATCH WEDGES

Cover each foundation piece with fabric strips as for traditional paper foundation piecing. To do this, turn over the foundation muslin so that the side without the drawn lines is facing upwards. Place a strip right side up in a position that covers a 'stripe' near the centre of the wedge, then pin a second strip face down with a raw edge aligned with a raw edge of the first strip. Turn the foundation piece over and machine stitch along the drawn line so that each fabric strip is caught in the seam. Turn over and trim the seam allowance to approximately ¼in (6mm), less near the point. Unfold the second strip so that the right side of the fabric is face up on the foundation piece and press. Pin on

the third strip, aligning the raw edge with the raw edge on the second strip. Turn over and machine stitch along the next drawn line on the muslin. Trim the seam allowance as before and press the strip open. Continue adding strips in this way until you reach the edge of the muslin, making sure the last strip covers the seam allowance on the foundation piece. Then add strips to the other side of the muslin, starting again at the centre.

Once you have covered all the foundation pieces with wedge-shaped patches, trim off any excess patch fabric to align with the edges of the muslin foundations. Then baste the patch strips along the long outside edges to the muslin, along the marked seam lines.

ASSEMBLING PATCHWORK WEDGES

Place the patchwork wedges right side down on the footstool and pin them together along the seam lines, adjusting to fit. Remove the cover and baste the seam lines – don't worry

about sewing all the way to the top points of the wedges as the button will cover the gap. Machine stitch the wedges together, trim the seam allowances if necessary, and press open.

FINISHING

We recommend that you have the patchwork cover professionally attached as it requires quite a bit of experience. Take your button mould and the fabric to cover it with you to the upholsterer and they will also cover this professionally for you when they cover the footstool.

If you have done upholstery before and want to attempt attaching the patchwork yourself, you will need the following: a 6in (15cm) long doll-making needle, strong button string, needle-nose pliers, a heavy-duty staple gun, and dark fabric to cover the bottom of the footstool.

If your footstool has screw-on feet, remove these. (You might want to paint unfinished feet with a colour that matches your patchwork.) Smooth the new cover over the footstool with the right side facing up. Then cover the button mould with your chosen fabric. Using the long doll-making needle, thread the button string down through the middle of the footstool. You must press down on the top of the footstool at the same time to make a deep dent. Using needle-nose pliers, reach up through the bottom hole to grab the needle. Pull through and staple the string in place on the bottom of the stool. Stretch the cover to the bottom and staple, making tucks in the fabric at regular intervals. Trim off the excess fabric past the staples. Cover the bottom with dark fabric. If your footstool has screw-on feet, poke holes through the dark fabric for the foot screws and screw the feet back on.

baby's corrugated quilt

Most of the fabrics in this quilt are men's shirting fabrics, but there are a few scraps of KAFFE FASSETT's *Blue-and-White Stripes* as well. If you are making the quilt from old shirts on their way to a secondhand shop just cut away the worn or stained areas first.

SIZE

The finished patchwork measures approximately 25in x 43in (63cm x 108cm).

Note that any measurements on the diagrams are for finished patch sizes, excluding the seam allowances.

INGREDIENTS

44–45in (112–114cm) wide 100% cotton fabrics (many shirting fabrics come wider, so adjust amounts accordingly):

• **Fabric A:** ⅛–¼yd (12–25cm) each of at least 15 different woven-stripe shirting fabrics predominantly with grey-blue stripes on white or ecru grounds, and one with narrow lavender and charcoal stripes on a white ground (same as binding)

• **Fabric B:** Scraps of mostly solid-coloured fabrics and a few monochromatic small-scale prints in rose pinks, aqua, papaya yellow, turquoise, lime and lavender

• **Fabric C:** ¼yd (25cm) of a woven stripe with narrow grey stripes on a white ground

• **Fabric D:** ⅛yd (12cm) of a pastel plaid in blues, yellow and lime

• **Backing fabric:** 1⅓yd (1.2m)

• **Binding fabric:** ½yd (46cm) extra of woven stripe with narrow lavender and charcoal stripes on a white ground for bias binding

• **Lightweight cotton batting:** 32in x 50in (81cm x 126cm)

• **Quilting thread:** White thread

CUTTING PATCHES

Quilt centre

220 square patches: Cut 220 squares 2½in x 2½in (6.5cm x 6.5cm) from fabric A.

Border

4 border strips: From fabric C, cut two strips 2in x 40½in (5.5cm x

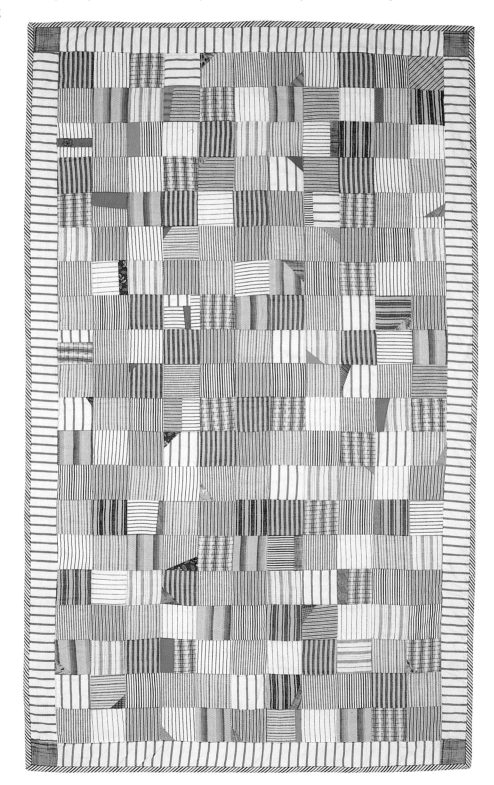

ASSEMBLY

Key
fabric A		fabric B		fabric C		fabric D

corner tabs and side strips, but the piecing should be random, so there is no need to match these shapes exactly.

26 squares with corner tabs: Take about 26 of the fabric-A 2½in (6.5cm) square patches and sew a randomly shaped fabric-B corner tab on to each patch. To do this, stitch a small scrap of fabric B to the square with right sides facing, then press open and trim off the excess to form a 2½in (6.5cm) pieced square.

14 squares with contrasting side strips: Take about 14 of the fabric-A 2½in (6.5cm) square patches and sew a straight or angled fabric-B strip along one side of each patch. Stitch on as for corner tabs, press and trim the pieced blocks to 2½in (6.5cm) squares.

101.5cm) and two strips 2in × 22½in (5.5cm × 56.5cm), all with the stripes running perpendicular to the long sides.

4 corner squares: Cut four squares 2in × 2in (5.5cm × 5.5cm) from fabric D.

MAKING PIECED BLOCKS
Make a total of about 45 pieced blocks, some with corner tabs and some with side strips as explained below. The assembly diagram shows the type of piecing shapes to use for

african weave throw

5 squares with striped side strips:
Take about five of the fabric-A 2½in (6.5cm) square patches and sew a straight strip in another fabric A on to each patch, joining the strip with the stripes running either in the same direction as the main patch *or* in the opposite direction. Stitch on as for the other pieced patches, press and trim the pieced blocks to 2½in (6.5cm) squares.

ASSEMBLING PATCHWORK
Quilt centre
Arrange the pieced squares and unpieced squares into 20 rows of 11 squares, with most of the stripes running parallel to the long sides of the quilt and the pieced blocks scattered around the patchwork. Arrange the squares on the floor or on a cotton-flannel design wall (see page 144).

Once you have achieved the desired effect, sew the squares together in rows, then join the rows, using a ¼in (7.5mm) seam allowance throughout.
Border
Sew one of the longer fabric-C strips to each side of the quilt centre. Sew a small fabric-D corner square to each end of the two remaining fabric-C strips, then join these strips to the top and bottom of the quilt.

FINISHING
Press the quilt top. Layer the quilt top, batting and backing; and baste (see page 148).

Using white thread, machine-quilt parallel lines from top to bottom of the quilt, stitching in-the-ditch between the squares. Then stitch in-the-ditch around the inner edge of the border.

Trim the quilt edges. Then cut the striped binding fabric on the bias and attach (see page 149).

All of the fabrics used in the *African Weave Throw* were taken from the KAFFE FASSETT Fabric Collection (see page 159). If you are choosing other fabrics to make a quilt with a similar look, aim for an overall effect of soft high colours.

SIZE
The finished patchwork measures approximately 63in × 63in (160cm × 160cm).
Note that any measurements on the diagrams are for finished patch sizes, excluding the seam allowances.

INGREDIENTS
45in (114cm) wide 100% cotton KAFFE FASSETT quilt fabrics:
• **Fabric A:** ½yd (46cm) of pink/purple *Ombré Stripe* (OS05) or a similar pink/purple and ecru ombré stripe
• **Fabric B:** ½yd (46cm) of green *Ombré Stripe* (OS01) or a similar sage green and ecru ombré stripe
• **Fabric C:** ½yd (46cm) of brown *Ombré Stripe* (OS04) or a similar soft brown and ecru ombré stripe
• **Fabric D:** ¾yd (70cm) of blue *Ombré Stripe* (OS02) or a similar blue and ecru ombré stripe
• **Fabric E:** ¾yd (70cm) of broad *Blue-and-White Stripe* (BWS02) or a similar broad, dusty blue and ecru stripe
• **Fabric F:** ¼yd (25cm) each of *Shot Cotton* in 'ginger' SC01, 'opal' SC05, 'tangerine' SC11, 'chartreuse' SC12, 'lavender' SC14, 'mustard' SC16, 'sage' SC17, 'tobacco' SC18, 'lichen' SC19,

'smoky' SC20 and 'duck egg blue' SC26, or a similar selection of 11 different solid-coloured fabrics in cool and warm shades
• **Fabric G:** ¾yd (70cm) of narrow *Blue-and-White Stripe* (BWS01) or a similar narrow, dusty blue and ecru woven stripe (see backing and binding fabrics)
• **Backing fabric:** 3½yd (3.2m) extra of fabric G
• **Binding fabric:** ½yd (46cm) extra of fabric G for bias binding
• **Lightweight cotton batting:** 71in × 71in (180cm × 180cm)
• **Quilting thread:** Beige thread
• **Templates:** Use templates W, X, Y and Z on pages 152, 153 and 157

CUTTING PATCHES
Quilt centre
When the square patches are cut from the striped fabrics, the stripes will not be in the same position on each square and will not match when joined – this is part of the design.
Fabric A (pink/purple ombré stripe): Cut 52 template-W squares from fabric A.

Fabric B (green ombré stripe): Cut 52 template-W squares from fabric B.

Fabric C (brown ombré stripe): Cut 50 template-W squares from fabric C.

Fabric D (blue ombré stripe): Cut 77 template-W squares from fabric D.

Fabric E (bold blue-and-white stripe): Cut 77 template-W squares from fabric E.

Fabric F (solids): Cut a total of 170 matching pairs of template-X triangles from fabric F, for a total of 340 triangles.

TEMPLATES

3in (7.5cm)

template W

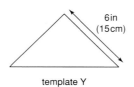

3in (7.5cm)

template X

6in (15cm)

template Y

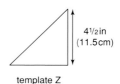

4½in (11.5cm)

template Z

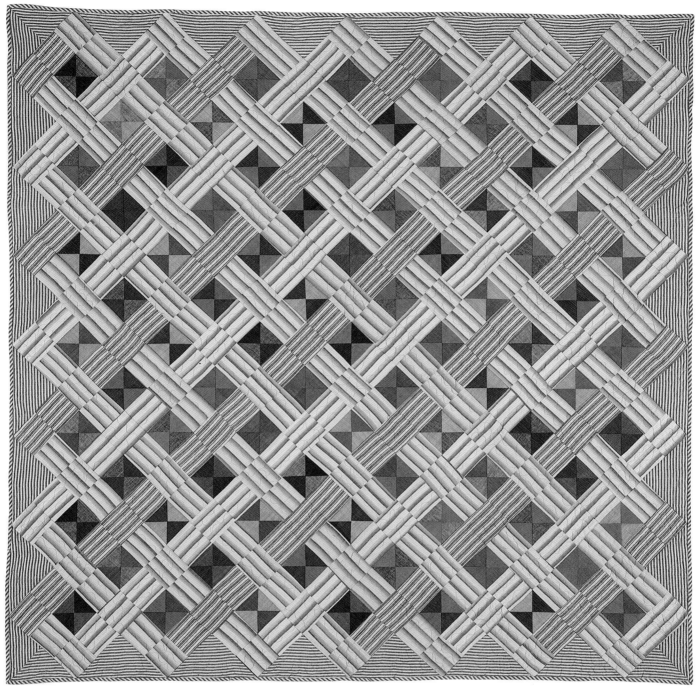

Border
Fabric G (narrow blue-and-white stripe): Cut 24 template-Y triangles

Four-triangle block

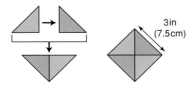

3in
(7.5cm)

and eight template-Z corner triangles from fabric G. (Make sure that the stripes run parallel to the long edge of each triangle following the grain lines marked on the templates.)

MAKING BLOCKS
85 four-triangle blocks: Make 85 four-triangle blocks, joining two pairs of matching fabric-F template-X triangles

as shown in the diagram. (Use the seam allowance marked on the templates throughout.)

ASSEMBLING PATCHWORK
Following the assembly diagram on page 142, arrange the blocks and patches for the quilt centre and border on the floor or on a cotton-flannel design wall (see page 144).

Make sure that the stripes on the striped squares follow the direction of the 'ribbon of stripes' that appears to weave in and out.

Sew the patches and blocks together in diagonal rows as shown, then join the rows.

FINISHING

Press the quilt top. Layer the quilt top, batting and backing; and baste (see page 148).

Using beige thread, machine-quilt as shown in the diagram.

Trim the quilt edges. Then cut the binding on the bias from fabric G (narrow blue-and-white stripe) and attach (see page 149).

Quilting for African Weave

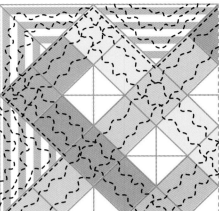

ASSEMBLY

Key

fabric A

fabric B

fabric C

fabric D

fabric E

fabric-F blocks

fabric G

going back to basics

The methods that follow are not meant to cover all the possible technical approaches to patchwork; they are merely the basics along with some very useful tips. Both hand piecing and machine piecing are covered. Those of you who want to carry your work with you may opt for the traditional hand piecing, but if you are keen on speedy results and have a sewing machine, you should try machine stitching your patchwork.

My advice is always the following – try not to get bogged down by the techniques. With practice the techniques will become second nature, and you will be able to enjoy concentrating on playing with colours within a patchwork geometry.

PATCHWORK FABRICS

One hundred per cent lightweight cotton fabrics, specially produced for quilts, are the best materials to use for patchwork. Their advantages are that they have a firm weave, are easy to cut, crease and press, and slow to fray. They also come in an astounding range of colours and prints, which means that the choice of palette is endless.

The delicious textures and soft, subtle shades of upholstery/furnishing fabrics do lend themselves to lovely patchworks (see the *Hat Boxes Quilt* on pages 24 and 25), but they are not as easy to handle as lightweight cotton, so are not recommended for beginners.

Liza and I are forever buying fabric for our stash. Just as an artist needs paints, the quiltmaker needs a palette of fabrics. One thing to remember, it to look out for odd-coloured fabrics to add to your collection. Certain colours are easy to find – like cherry reds or navy blues – but if you come across an unusual greeny beige or chalky periwinkle, snatch up a quarter or a half a yard (25–50cm) to add to your palette. Stripes are also handy to collect for bias binding quilts – you'll need about ¾yd (70cm) for a bias binding for a bed-size quilt.

Scrap fabrics

In most of my patchwork designs, I like to use as many different fabrics as possible in order to make the colour composition interesting and lively. This makes the designs especially suited to the use of scrap fabrics, leftover pieces big enough for several patches.

If you are a keen patchwork-quilter, you will already have a collection of scraps that you are just waiting for the perfect opportunity to use up. Once you have chosen the quilt you want to make, my advice would be to start assembling the colours you will need by going through your remnants. Add to this by purchasing small amounts of the missing colours, or even by finding suitable one hundred per cent cotton dresses, blouses or shirts in charity/thrift shops or jumble sales. Remember that polyester is more difficult to quilt than pure cotton and is crease resistant, which is not a useful asset for patchwork.

Fabric colours and patterns

Each set of instructions for the quilts in this book gives fabric descriptions that are meant to be a guide to choosing fabrics. Read the descriptions and study the photography carefully to decide on your fabric palette.

Many of the designs make use of monochromatic prints or tone-on-tone prints. These prints are composed of one colour in two or more tones – such as a mid and dark blue pattern on a light blue ground or a light blue pattern on a mid blue ground, etc. At a distance small-scale monochromatic prints can appear to be solid colours but have a much more interesting effect than solid-coloured fabrics. The patterns soften and add visual 'texture' to the patchwork geometry.

Many of the designs also use prints composed of three or more colours, such as the large-scale floral and leaf prints in the *Garden* quilts (see pages 27–31). Even multi-coloured prints like these usually have a colour that

predominates, so pay attention to this hue when selecting them. Alternatively, you can use only the areas of the print that suit your colour scheme, for example by framing the patches over the yellow flowers or only over the magenta flowers in a bold multi-coloured floral.

Always look at multi-coloured prints from a distance before buying them. For example, you may be looking for a fabric that is predominantly blue, you find one that looks blue with tiny yellow flowers, but when you stand away from it that perfect floral turns green!

Not only prints, but also stripes, plaids and polka dots can enliven a patchwork design. In some quilts, using all of these types of fabric pattern together definitely enhances the overall effect. Don't shy away from stripes because you think they may be hard to cut straight or match. There is no need to match stripes in patchwork, and there is no harm in the stripes being slightly off kilter – in fact this can actually be done on purpose for an interesting effect.

The only thing to remember when mixing fabrics is that they should all be about the same weight, and if you stick to materials specially made for quilts this will not be a problem as they are generally all the same lightweight, one hundred per cent cotton.

Fabric quantities

Giving fabric amounts for a patchwork that uses a variety of prints is unfortunately not an exact science, and quantities in instructions should only be considered an approximate guide. It is better to have too much fabric than too little and too many different prints than too few; excess can always be used up in future projects. Some of the instructions in this book give approximate amounts for the patches and others use so many different fabrics that a variety of scraps are recommended.

Keep in mind that running out of a particular fabric is not a tragedy – think of it as a design opportunity. Look for a fabric with a similar feel and use it to finish the job. One of the reasons antique quilts are so wonderful is the make-do philosophy of the makers. Those old quirky colour combinations born out of a make-do process are charming indeed.

If you are calculating exact amounts for borders, bindings or backings, remember that although specially made patchwork fabrics are usually 44in to 45in (about 112cm to 114cm) wide the usable width is only about 42in to 43in (107cm to 109cm) due to slight shrinkage and the necessary removal of selvedges.

Fabric preparation

Always prewash cotton fabric before cutting it into patch shapes. This is a good test for colourfastness and also, if necessary, preshrinks the fabric. Be sure to wash darks and lights separately. Begin by soaking the fabric in hot soapy water for a few minutes, then look at the water to see if any colour has bled out. To be absolutely sure that the fabric is colourfast, press the wet fabric between white paper towels to check for bleeding.

Rinse the fabric well and when it is still damp, press it with a hot iron. After pressing, cut off the selvedges with a rotary cutter. (See right for more detailed information about this cutting tool.)

TOOLS AND EQUIPMENT

Very few tools are needed for patchwork. If you have a sewing workbox, you will probably already have the essentials – fabric scissors, pins, needles, a ruler, tape measure, ironing board and iron. This is all you need if you are making a simple 'squares' patchwork.

For more complicated patch shapes you will need templates. These can be bought in various sizes or you can make your own. For this you will need graph paper, a ruler, a pencil, a pair of paper scissors or a craft knife, and for the template itself a piece of thin, stiff cardboard or specially made template plastic.

Probably the most useful patchwork tool to appear this century is the

rotary cutter. With a rotary cutter, rotary ruler and rotary cutting board you can cut patches in straight accurate lines in a fraction of the time it takes with scissors. New gadgets for making patchwork quilts are always coming on the market and you should keep your eye out for anything you think will save you time and effort.

For machine piecing, of course, you will need a sewing machine. Quilting can also be done on a machine and requires a machine with a 'walking' or darning foot.

Tools for designing

There are two invaluable tools that Liza and I use for designing: a design wall and a reducing glass. It is possible to arrange a full size patchwork quilt on the floor, but when the floor space just isn't available or if you need to be able to step back far enough to get a full view of the whole thing, a design wall covered with cotton flannel is just the thing.

Our design wall is large enough for working on a queen-size bed cover and is made with two 4ft by 8ft (about 122cm by 244cm) sheets of insulation board. Insulation board is a very light board about ¾in (2cm) thick; it has a foam core that is covered on one side with paper and on the other with foil. You could use any sturdy, lightweight board like this, but insulation board is especially handy as it can be cut with a craft knife. To make yourself a design wall, cover the two boards on one side with a good quality cotton flannel in a neutral colour such as dull light brown, taupe or medium grey. Then join the boards with three 'hinges' using a strong adhesive tape. Stick the hinges to the back of the boards so that you can fold the flannel sides together. The hinges will also allow you to bend the design wall slightly so it will stand by itself. If you need to put the wall away with a design in progress on it, just place paper over the arranged patches, fold the boards together and slide them under a bed.

A quilter's reducing glass looks like a magnifying glass but it makes things

smaller. It helps you to see how a fabric print or even a whole patchwork layout will look at a distance. Somehow, seeing the quilt layout reduced makes the errors in the design just pop out and become very obvious. Reducing glasses are widely available in shops that sell patchwork supplies. Looking through a camera can be an acceptable substitute.

PREPARING PATCHES

Once you have chosen all the fabrics for your quilt and prepared them (see above), you are ready to start cutting patches. The instructions for each quilt in this book show all the patch shapes used. This will give you a good idea of how complicated or simple a patchwork will be to cut and piece.

Patches for designs made entirely of squares can be cut quickly and accurately with a rotary cutter, whereas triangle, parallelogram or trapezoid patch shapes will usually require templates for accurate cutting.

Rotary cutting

Rotary cutting is especially useful for cutting accurate square patches and for cutting quilt border strips. The rotary mats and transparent acrylic rulers come in a range of sizes. Although it is handy to have a range of large and small mats and rulers, if you want to start out with just one mat and one ruler, choose an 18in by 24in (46cm by 61cm) mat and a 6in by 24in (15cm by 61cm) ruler. With a mat and ruler this size you can cut both border strips and patches with ease. The ruler will have measurement division markings on it as well as 90-, 60- and 45-degree angles.

Before beginning to rotary cut, first press out any creases or fold marks on your fabric. Rotary-cut strips are usually cut across the fabric width from selvedge to selvedge, so you will need to straighten the raw end. Aligning the selvedges, fold the fabric in half lengthways and smooth it out. Keeping the selvedges together, fold the fabric in half again bringing the selvedges to the fold. On 44in (112cm) wide fabric there will now be an 11in (28cm) long edge to cut strips across.

Place the cutting board under the folded fabric and line up the selvedges with a line on the cutting board. Overlap the acrylic rotary ruler about ½in (12mm) over the raw edge of the fabric, using the lines on the cutting board to make sure that the ruler is perfectly perpendicular to the selvedges. Pressing down on the ruler and the cutter, roll the cutter away from you along the edge of the ruler. When using a rotary cutter, try to manipulate the fabric as little as possible. Careful cutting means you won't have to compensate for uneven edges while sewing and can relax more.

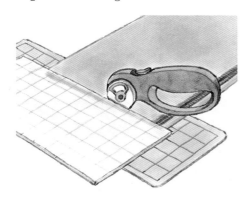

To cut a strip with a rotary cutter, first trim the raw edge of the folded fabric (see above), then align this trimmed edge with the markings on the ruler, keeping the ruler firmly in place and rolling the cutter away from you. Check intermittently to make sure that the raw edge is aligned with the correct position on the ruler.

To cut patches, first cut a strip the width of the square, then cut the strip into squares by aligning the ruler markings to the correct measurement (see above). For speed in cutting, stick

a piece of masking tape on the wrong side of the ruler along the measurement line that corresponds to the patch size.

With practice you will be able to cut up to six layers of fabric with a large rotary cutter, thereby cutting several patches at once. Just remember to change the cutter blade as soon as it shows the slightest hint of dulling.

Making templates

For patch shapes other than squares and strips, you will need a template of the shape to draw on to the fabric or cut around. Standard-sized templates are available in shops that sell patchwork fabrics and tools.

You can also make your own templates. The best material for a template is clear template plastic. Although it is easy to cut, it is very durable and will retain its shape despite being traced around time after time. Its other advantage it its transparency – you can see through it to frame fabric motifs. Thin, stiff cardboard can also be used if template plastic is not available.

To make a template, first trace the template shape provided with the quilt instructions either directly on to template plastic, or on to a piece of tracing paper and then on to thin cardboard. Use a ruler for drawing the straight lines, and transfer the cutting line, the seam line and the grain line. Cut out the template.

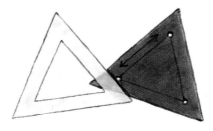

Punch a hole in each corner at each pivot point on the seam line using a ⅛in (3mm) hole punch. This type of template is suitable for machine-pieced patches (see above right). For hand-pieced patches, you should ideally draw the seam line on the fabric and not the cutting line. The

seam allowance can then be cut by eye around the patch. You may find that it adds to the accuracy of either machine or hand piecing to draw both the seam line and the cutting line on the fabric. For this you will need to make a window template from template plastic (see above left). A window template is basically just a frame as wide as the seam allowance.

Before going on to cut all your patches, make a patchwork block with test pieces to check the accuracy of your templates. This is especially important with blocks that require inset seams.

Cutting template patches

To cut template patches, place the template face down on the wrong side of the fabric, aligning the grain line arrow with the straight grain of the fabric (the crossways or the lengthways grain).

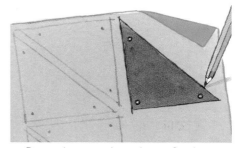

Press the template down firmly with one hand and draw around it with a sharp pencil in the other hand (see above). Position the patches as close together as possible or even touching in order to save fabric.

You may notice when cutting patches from striped fabrics that although you are drawing around the patches on the straight grain, the outlines do not run exactly with the stripes. Do not worry about this. This will hardly be noticeable once the patches are pieced, and if it is, it just adds to the handmade quality of the patchwork.

Cutting reverse template patches

A reverse template is the mirror image of a patch shape. If the instructions call for a template and the reverse of that template, the same

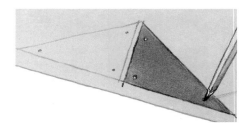

template is used for both shapes.

For the reverse of a template, lay the template face up on the wrong side of the fabric. Draw around the template in the usual way (see above).

BASIC HAND AND MACHINE PIECING

Patches can be joined together by hand or machine. Although machine stitching is much quicker, you might like the idea of being able to carry your patches around with you and work on them in every spare moment. Choose whichever method you find more enjoyable.

Arranging cut patches

Quilt instructions always give a layout for how to arrange the various patch shapes to form the overall geometrical design. It is, of course, possible to just pick your cut patches at random and stitch them together as you pull them out of the pile; but you will achieve a much better effect if you plan your colour arrangement before beginning to piece the patches together.

Lay the patches out on the floor or stick them to a large board covered with cotton flannel (see Tools and Equipment), then step back and study the effect. If you don't have access to such a large area, you can arrange individual blocks and, after the blocks have been stitches, arrange the completed blocks on the floor until you are satisfied with the layout.

Creating a stunning colour composition is the most important part of the whole process of patchwork. You will notice that both the colour itself and its value will come into play in your arrangement. The value of a colour is its tone – which ranges from very light tones through to dark. Colours also have relative brightnesses, from dusty and

dull to radiant and jewel-like. Dull colours appear greyer than others and tend to recede, while bright, intense colours stand out.

Make sure the colour arrangement is just right before starting to stitch the pieces together. Leave it for a few days and then come back to it and try another arrangement, or try replacing colours that do not seem to work together with new shades. Don't be afraid to position 'mistake' patches inside the arrangement to keep it lively and unpredictable. An unpredictable arrangement will always have more energy and life than one that follows a strict light/dark format.

If the quilt has no border or simply an uncomplicated strip border, it will be easy to change the size of the quilt at this point; but remember to cut any strip borders to the new size.

Machine piecing

If you have a sewing machine, you'll be able to achieve quick results by machine piecing your patches together. Follow the instructions for the order in which to piece the individual patchwork blocks and then assemble the blocks together in rows.

The most important piecing tip for beginners is that you should use the same neutral-coloured thread to piece your entire patchwork. Taupe or light grey thread will work for most patchworks, except when the overall scheme is either very dark or very light. Be sure to purchase one hundred per cent cotton thread.

Pin the patches together, right sides facing, and matching the seam lines and corner points carefully. (You may find that you can stitch small squares together without pinning, so try both ways.) Then machine stitch, using the correct seam allowance and removing each pin before the needle reaches it. Except for inset seams, machine stitched patchwork seams are sewn from raw edge to raw edge. (There is no need to work backstitches at the beginning and end of each patch, since the stitches will be secured by crossing seam lines as the pieces are joined together.)

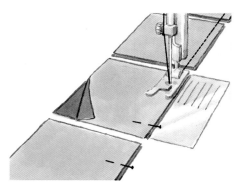

You can save both time and thread by chain piecing. This is done by feeding through the pinned together pieces one after another without lifting the presser foot. Let the machine stitch in the air a few times before it reaches the next pair of patches (see above).

Pressing patch seams

After each seam has been stitched and before opening out the pieces, press the seams flat to imbed the stitches. Then, if the patches have been chain pieced, cut them apart. Next, open out the patches and press the seam allowances to one side.

Continue joining the patches into blocks, then the blocks into rows as directed, pressing all the seam allowances in one row in the same direction. After all the blocks are joined into rows, join the rows together.

Try to press the seam allowances in every alternate row in the opposite direction so that you don't have to stitch through two layers of seam allowances when joining the rows together.

Hand piecing blocks

Hand stitching your patches together is time-consuming, but it does give a beautiful handmade finish to the patchwork.

To hand piece two patches, pin them right sides together so that the pencilled seam lines are facing outwards. Using a single strand of thread, secure the end with a couple of backstitches (see next page, top). Then work short, even running stitches along the seam line, beginning and ending at the seam-line corners

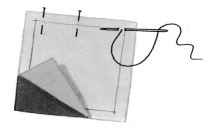

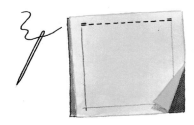

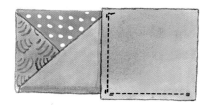

(see above). When hand piecing, never stitch across the seam allowances. End the seam with two backstitches.

Press the seam allowances to one side as for machine-pieced seams, or press all seam allowances open.

Stitching inset seams

You will find that most patches can be joined together with a straight seam line, but with some patchwork layouts a patch will need to be sewn into a corner formed by two other patches. This will require a seam line that turns a corner – this types of seam is called an inset seam.

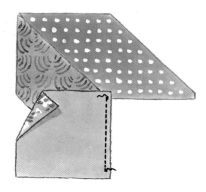

First, align the patches along one side of the angle and pin, matching up the corner points exactly. Machine stitch along the seam line of this edge up to the corner point and work a few backstitches to secure (see above).

Then pivot the set-in patch, align the adjacent side with the edge of the next patch and pin. Beginning exactly

at the corner point, work a few backstitches to secure, then machine stitch along the seam line to the outer edge of the next patch and pin. Beginning exactly at the corner point, work a few backstitches to secure, then machine stitch along the seam line to the outer edge of the patches (see above).

Trim away excess fabric from the seam allowance at the corner of the inset patch as necessary. Press the new seams, easing the corner into the correct shape (see above).

APPLIQUÉ

Several quilts in this book use the technique of appliqué. Appliqué is the addition of shaped fabric pieces on top of a backing fabric. Templates are provided for the shapes.

The edges of appliqué motifs are usually either turned under, as on the *Dark Rice Bowls* wall hanging on page 15, or the raw edges are covered with machine embroidery as on the *Hat Boxes Quilt* on page 25 and the *Pastel Bubbles* patchwork on page 19. Two other less common techniques are covering the raw edges with a bias binding as on the *Suzanni Quilt* on

page 23 or leaving the raw edges exposed as on the *Squares Window Blind* on page 42.

Whichever method you are using for your appliqué, be sure to cut the shapes from well pressed fabric. Using spray starch on the fabric beforehand can make cutting easier and keep the fabric from fraying too quickly. Use very sharp scissors when cutting the appliqué pieces and do not handle them too much once they are cut. Keep them flat until you need them.

If you are using machine blanket, buttonhole or satin stitch to cover the raw edges of appliqué and secure it to the backing, pin and baste the fabric shapes to your patchwork first. It is also a good idea to place sewing stabilizer paper behind the backing, as it helps the fabric slide neatly through the machine. The same applies to other machine stitch methods for applying appliqué.

Turning under the edges of appliqué is more difficult. A hem allowance of ¼in (6mm) is added all around the finished shape. This hem allowance is then notched or clipped where necessary along curves or at corners, and turned to the wrong side. As an aid to turning hems, you can use freezer paper. Just cut a piece of freezer paper to the size of the finished appliqué shape and press the waxy side of the paper to the wrong side of the appliqué piece. Then press the hem allowance to the wrong side over the paper, and remove the paper. The appliqué is then ready to be pinned and basted to the patchwork, and finally stitched in place by hand or machine.

Once you have stitched your appliqué to the patchwork backing, cut away the backing behind the appliqué to within ¼in (6mm) of the seam. This keeps the fabric from becoming too bulky and keeps the colour of the backing from showing through.

QUILTING AND FINISHING

After you have finished piecing your patchwork, press it carefully. It is now ready to be quilted if quilting is required. However, many items of patchwork, such as cushion covers, throws, curtains and table covers need only be backed.

Quilting patterns

Quilting is the stitching that joins together the three layers of the quilt sandwich – top, batting/wadding and backing. For patchworks that have a strong design story of their own, you may want to chose a quilting pattern that does not detract from the patchwork. In some instances, you will find that stitch-in-the-ditch quilting is the perfect choice, since the quilting lines are stitched into the patch seams making the quilting stitches invisible on the right side of the patchwork.

Outline quilting is another simple quilting pattern that will suit many patchwork designs. It is worked by stitching ¼in (6mm) from the patch seam lines.

You will need to mark more complicated quilting patterns on the right side of the pieced patchwork before the quilt layers are joined. The marking can be done with specially designed quilting markers. Using a quilting stencil is the easiest way to mark a complicated pattern on to the fabric. These stencils are widely available in shops that sell patchwork and quilting materials.

If you are in doubt about which quilting pattern to chose, test the pattern on a spare pieced block. This will also be a good way to check whether you chosen quilting thread is a suitable colour. Quilting thread is a specially made cotton thread that is thicker and stronger than ordinary sewing thread. The thread colour should usually blend invisibly into the overall colour of the patchwork quilt when it is viewed from a distance.

Preparing the backing and batting

Most large quilts need about 6–8yd (5.5–7.3m) of backing fabric. Liza and I are not fans of plain muslin on the quilt backs and prefer a print or stripe that looks good with the front. Liza tries to find half-price fabrics for backings.

To prepare the backing fabric, first cut the selvedges off, then seam the pieces together to form a backing at least 3in (7.5cm) bigger all around than the patchwork. It is best to join the pieces so that the seam lines run lengthways.

If the batting/wadding has been rolled, unroll it and let it rest before cutting it to about the same size as the backing. Batting comes in various thicknesses, but a pure cotton or mixed cotton and polyester batting that is fairly thin will be a good choice for most quilts. Thicker batting is usually only suitable when the quilt layers are being tied together. A hundred per cent cotton batting will give your quilt the attractive, relatively flat appearance of an antique quilt.

Basting the quilt layers

Lay out the backing wrong side up and smooth it out. Place the batting on top of the backing, then lay the pieced patchwork right side up on top of the batting and smooth it out.

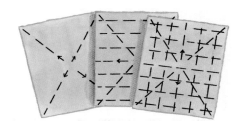

Beginning at the centre, baste two diagonal lines from corner to corner through the layers (see above left). Make stitches about 3in (7.5cm) long and try not to lift the layers too much as you stitch. Then, again always beginning at the centre and working outwards, baste horizontal and vertical lines across the layers (see above centre and right). The basting lines should be about 4in (10cm) apart.

Hand quilting

Hand quilting is best done with the quilt layers mounted in a quilting frame or hoop. Thread a short quilting needle (an 8 to 11 'between') with an 18in (46cm) length of special cotton quilting thread and knot the end. With the quilt top facing upwards and beginning at the centre of the basted quilt layers, insert the needle through the top about ½in (12mm) from the starting point and into the batting, then bring it out at the starting point. Pull the thread to pop the knot into the batting.

Loading about three or four stitches on to the needle and working with one hand under the quilt to help the needle back up again, make short, even running stitches. Pull the thread through and continue along the quilting line in this way.

It is more important to make even stitches on both sides of the quilt than to make small ones. When the thread is about to run out, make a small backstitch, then pierce this backstitch to anchor it and run the thread end through into the batting.

Machine quilting

For machine quilting, use a walking foot for straight lines and a darning foot for curved lines. Use regular sewing thread and choose a colour that blends with the overall colour of the patchwork for the top thread and one that matches the backing for the bobbin thread. Begin and end the quilting lines with very short stitches to secure, leaving long ends to thread into the batting later. Follow the machine manual for tips on using the walking or darning feet.

Tying quilts

If you don't have the time needed for allover quilting, you can tie together the basted layers of your patchwork quilt. Make sure that you are using a batting with a high loft, because thin cotton battings usually require quite close quilting lines.

Use a sharp needle with a large eye, and wool yarn, thick embroidery thread or narrow ribbon for the tying. For simple tying, cut a 7in (18cm) length of yarn and thread the needle.

Beginning the tying at the centre of the quilt, make a small stitch through all three layers. Tie the two ends of the yarn into a double knot and trim (see previous page, bottom). If you are making bows, use a longer length.

Binding quilt edges

Once the quilt has been quilted or tied together, remove the basting threads. Then baste around the quilt just under ¼in (about 5mm) from the edge of the patchwork. Trim the outer edge of the quilt, cutting away the excess batting and backing right up to the edge of the patchwork and, if necessary, straightening the edge of the patchwork in the process.

Cut 2in (5cm) wide binding strips either on the straight grain or on the bias. (Striped fabrics look especially effective when cut on the bias to form diagonal stripes around the edge of the patchwork.) Join these binding strips end-to-end with diagonal seams until the strip is long enough to fit around the edge.

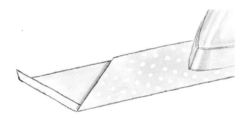

Cut the beginning end of the binding strip at a 45-degree angle, turn ¼in (6mm) to the wrong side along this cut end, and press. Then fold the strip in half lengthways with the wrong sides together and press (see above).

Place the doubled binding on the right side of the quilt (see above), with the longer side of the left-hand

end facing the quilt and the raw edges aligned. Stitch from the second folded edge on the binding ¼in (6mm) from the edge, up to ¼in (6mm) from the first corner. Make a few backstitches and cut the thread ends.

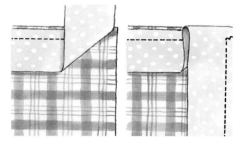

Fold the binding up, making a 45-degree angle (see above left). Keeping the diagonal fold in place, fold the binding back down and align the edge with the next side of the quilt. Beginning at the point where the last stitching ended, stitch down the next side (see above right).

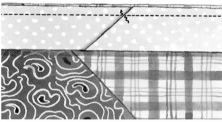

Continue stitching the binding in place all around the edge in this way, tucking the end inside the beginning of the binding (see above).

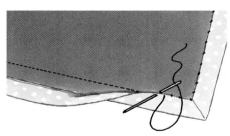

Turn the folded edge of the binding to the back. Hand stitch in place, folding a mitre at each corner (see above).

USING ANTIQUE BLOCKS

Many people who buy antique quilt tops and blocks like to use them in a

historically correct manner, purchasing vintage fabrics to fix damaged areas and to complete the project. This is one approach to using old pieces of patchwork. Liza and I, however, prefer to integrate antique blocks with new fabrics and give them an up-to-date twist. You can see our approach in *Medallion Circles*, *Granny's Flower Garden* and *String Stars* on pages 6, 9 and 11. The backgrounds used for our old patchwork pieces are not meant to showcase the blocks, but rather to meld with the blocks and form a lively combination.

Preparing the blocks

Antique patchwork pieces are not always in perfect condition or absolutely flat, but don't let this deter you from integrating them into a new quilt. First, press the old blocks as flat as possible, then trim them to the exact size and shape you need.

To repair a hole or slit in antique fabric, you can make a 'bandage' from a small patch of a similarly coloured fabric with fusible web attached to it. Iron the patch behind the tear or slit. Alternatively, carefully appliqué a similar fabric over the hole.

Stitching to a new background

When all the necessary repairs have been made, the blocks are ready to be appliquéd to a background made up of new fabrics. We sometimes tea dye new background fabrics that appear too clean and crisp to meld in with the old blocks. Be sure to test this on a scrap before dunking new fabric.

If your antique block is not perfectly flat, make little tucks to smooth it out while stitching it to the new ground. Once the blocks are all in place, do not cut away the backing behind them; this new base fabric acts as a stabilizer for the old materials. Quilting over any remaining lumps in old blocks will further flatten them.

Adding borders

For borders, use more antique blocks if you have suitable ones, or make new ones that echo the elements in the old pieces at the centre of your quilt.

tracing the templates

The templates for the patchworks are given on pages 150–157. They are all shown actual size, except for those for the *Dark Rice Bowls* and the *Hat Boxes Quilt* which need to be enlarged. The solid lines indicate the finished size of the templates and the broken lines the seam allowances. Some of letters are used more than once for templates so be sure to find the one you need for the specific quilt you are making.

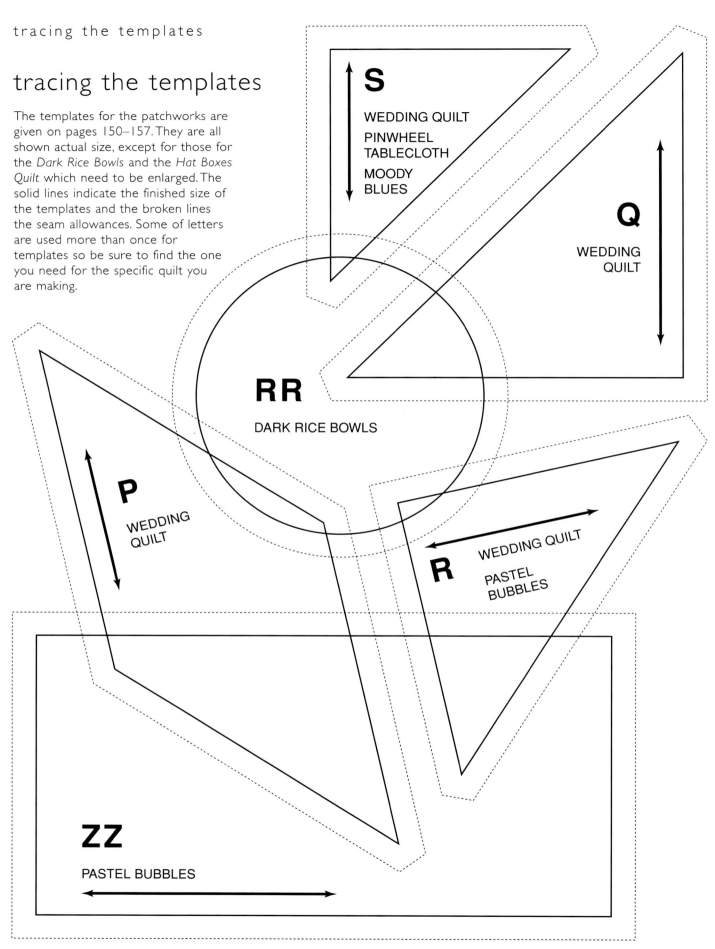

S
WEDDING QUILT
PINWHEEL
TABLECLOTH
MOODY
BLUES

Q
WEDDING
QUILT

RR
DARK RICE BOWLS

P
WEDDING
QUILT

R
WEDDING QUILT

PASTEL
BUBBLES

ZZ
PASTEL BUBBLES

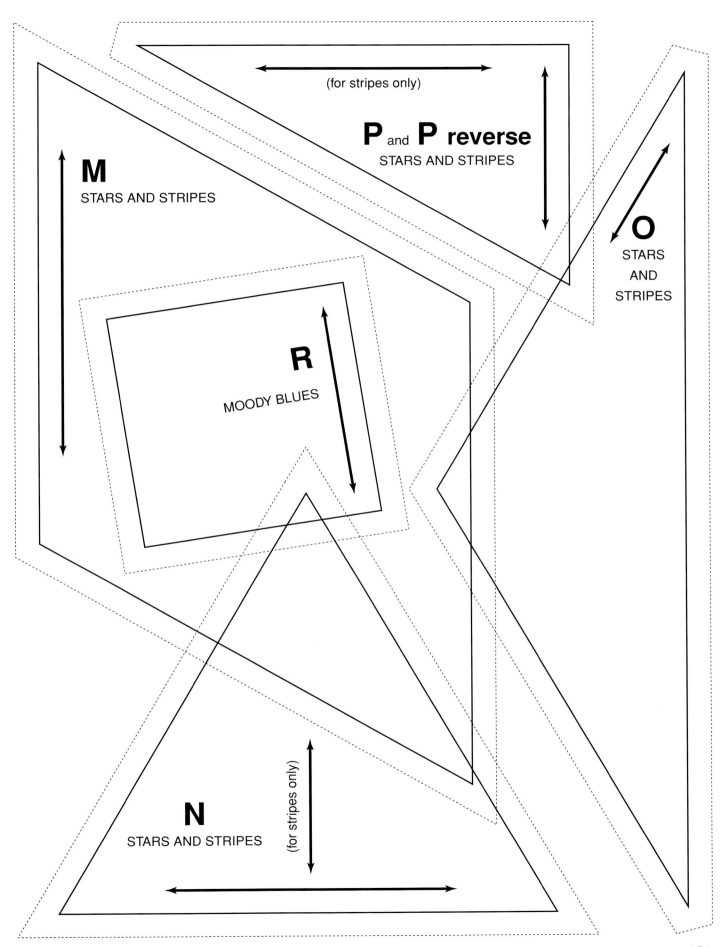

M
STARS AND STRIPES

P and **P reverse**
STARS AND STRIPES

(for stripes only)

O
STARS
AND
STRIPES

R
MOODY BLUES

N
STARS AND STRIPES

(for stripes only)

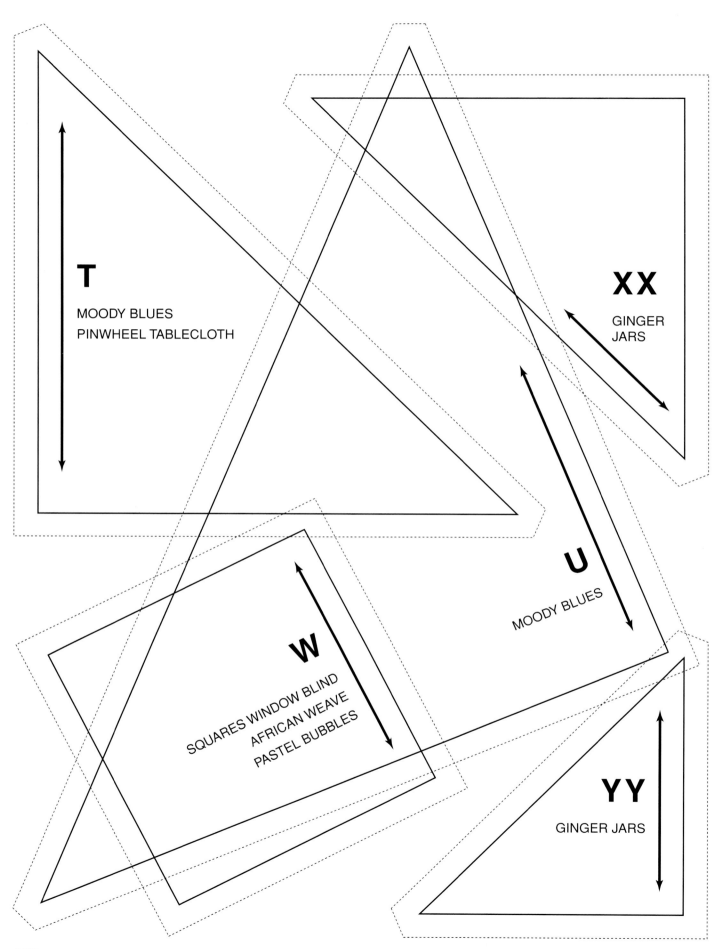

T

MOODY BLUES
PINWHEEL TABLECLOTH

XX

GINGER
JARS

U

MOODY BLUES

W

SQUARES WINDOW BLIND
AFRICAN WEAVE
PASTEL BUBBLES

YY

GINGER JARS

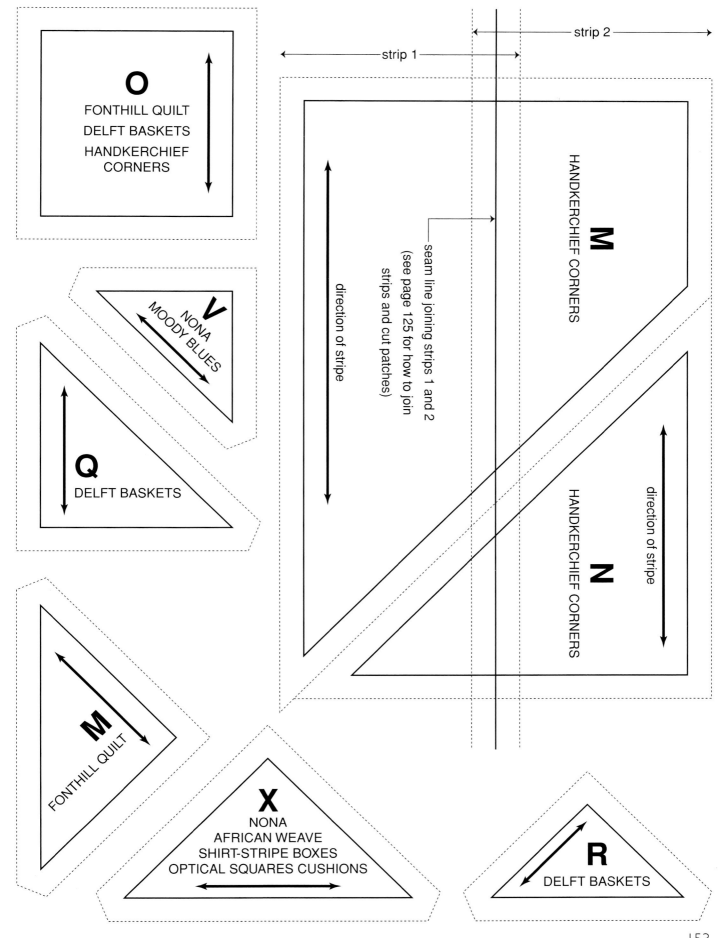

O
FONTHILL QUILT
DELFT BASKETS
HANDKERCHIEF CORNERS

strip 1

strip 2

M
HANDKERCHIEF CORNERS

seam line joining strips 1 and 2
(see page 125 for how to join
strips and cut patches)

direction of stripe

V
NONA
MOODY BLUES

Q
DELFT BASKETS

N
HANDKERCHIEF CORNERS

direction of stripe

M
FONTHILL QUILT

X
NONA
AFRICAN WEAVE
SHIRT-STRIPE BOXES
OPTICAL SQUARES CUSHIONS

R
DELFT BASKETS

DARK RICE BOWLS

The instructions for the *Dark Rice Bowls* start on page 72. The templates and appliqué shapes for the patchwork are shown here at 66 per cent of their actual size; enlarge 150 per cent for the correct size. Templates PP and QQ are overlapped and shown in the positions they will be in once sewn together; this is so that the appliqué can be shown in its final position. Once enlarged, the block below should measure 12in x 10in (30.5cm x 25.5cm) including the seam allowance around the outside of the block. For how to make appliqué templates with hem allowances for this project, see page 73.

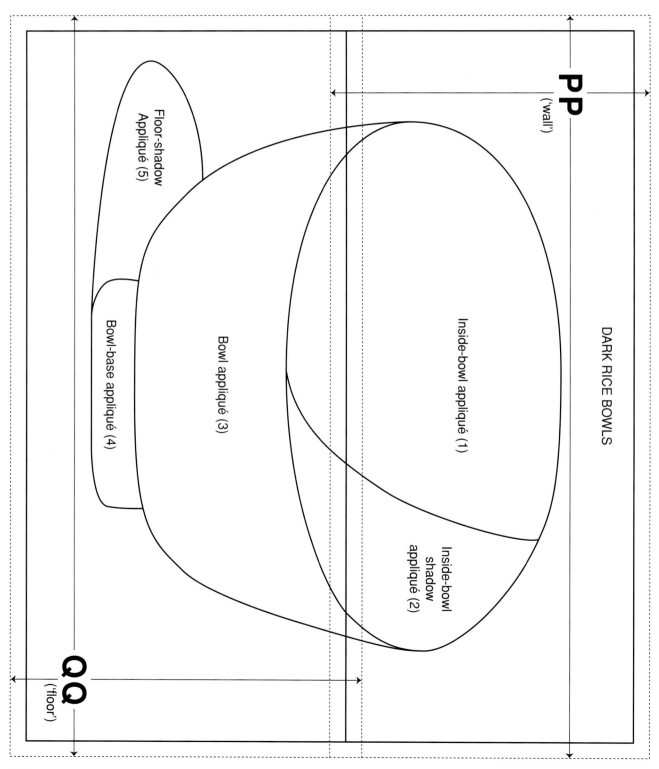

Floor-shadow Appliqué (5)

Bowl-base appliqué (4)

Bowl appliqué (3)

Inside-bowl appliqué (1)

Inside-bowl shadow appliqué (2)

PP ('wall')

QQ ('floor')

DARK RICE BOWLS

HAT BOXES QUILT

The instructions for the *Hat Boxes Quilt* start on page 83. The templates and appliqué shapes for the quilt are shown here at 50 per cent of their actual size; enlarge 200 per cent for the correct size. Templates K (square), J and J reverse (trapezoids) are overlapped and shown in the positions they will be in once sewn together; this is so that the appliqué can be shown in its final position.

Once enlarged, the hat box block below should measure 12½in x 12½in (31.7cm x 31.7cm) including the seam allowance.

See page 84 for how to cut and sew on the appliqué pieces.

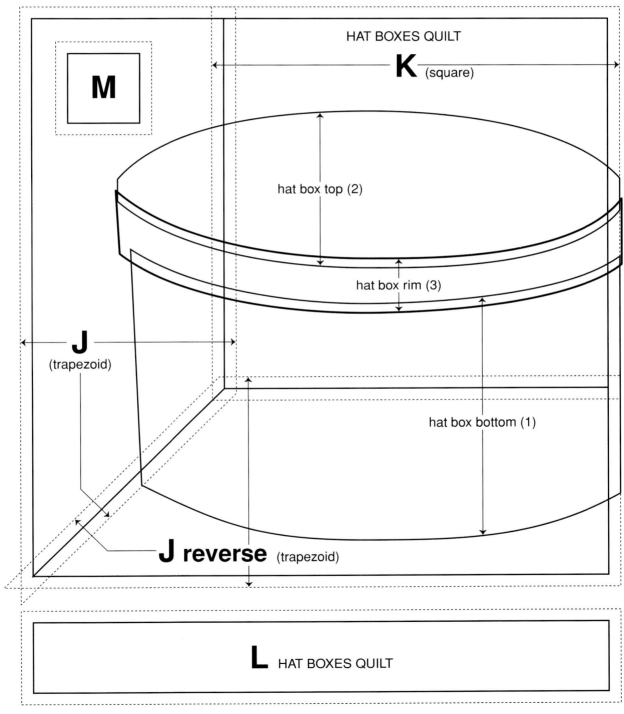

M

HAT BOXES QUILT

K (square)

hat box top (2)

hat box rim (3)

hat box bottom (1)

J (trapezoid)

J reverse (trapezoid)

L HAT BOXES QUILT

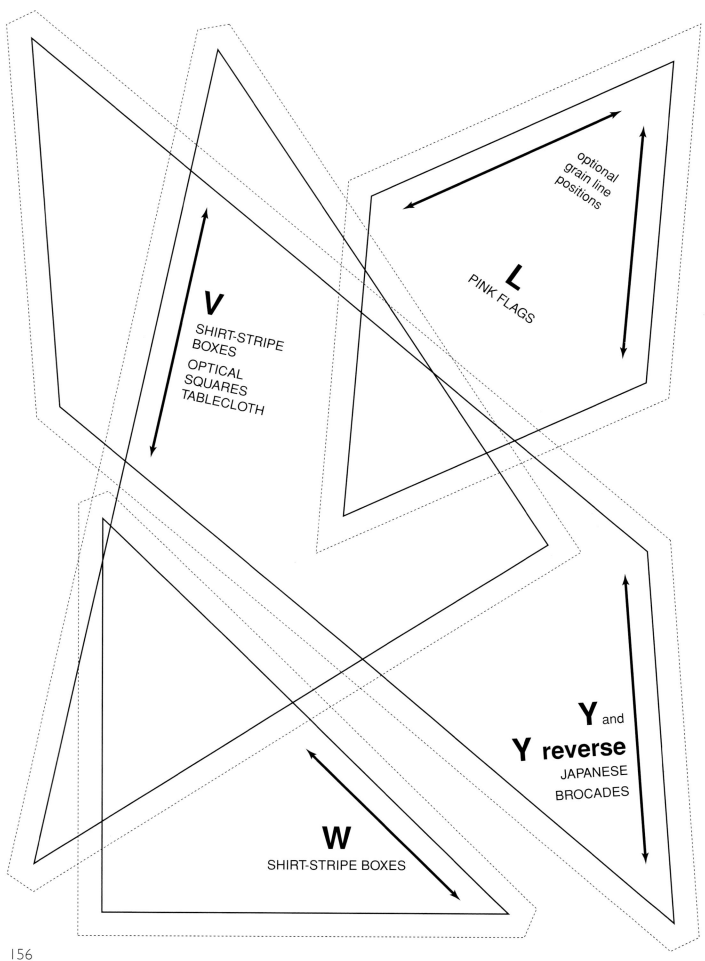

optional
grain line
positions

L

PINK FLAGS

V

SHIRT-STRIPE
BOXES

OPTICAL
SQUARES
TABLECLOTH

Y and
Y reverse

JAPANESE

BROCADES

W

SHIRT-STRIPE BOXES

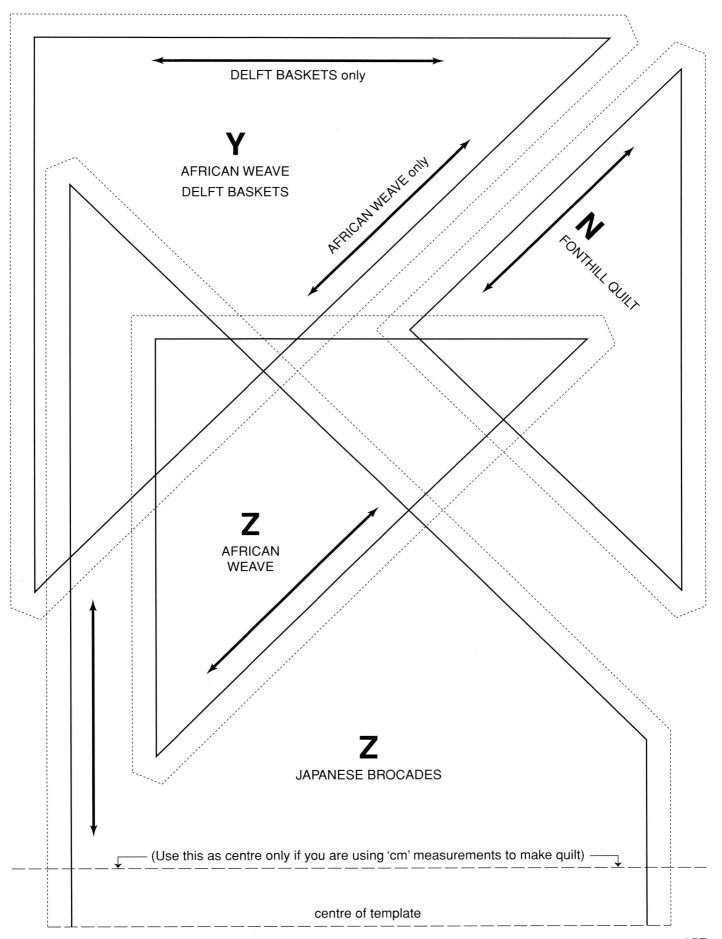

DELFT BASKETS only

Y
AFRICAN WEAVE
DELFT BASKETS

AFRICAN WEAVE only

N
FONTHILL QUILT

Z
AFRICAN
WEAVE

Z
JAPANESE BROCADES

(Use this as centre only if you are using 'cm' measurements to make quilt)

centre of template

acknowledgments

Kaffe Fassett and Liza Prior Lucy would like to acknowledge the help of the following people—

Thanks so much to the fabulous quilters who finished all of the quilts – Judy Irish and Cara Gulati.

Thanks to the piecers who made quilt tops – Penny Armagost, Andrea Graham, Cara Gulati, Faye Lucas, Rebekah Lynch, Meg Maas, Yvonne Mably, Judy Melson, Patricia Petrie, Kim Rowe, Anne Soriero, Pauline Smith and Janet Stoner.

Thanks to those lending a hand – Bonnie Adams, Maxine Farkas, Lois Griffin, Bobbi Penniman, Anne Pietropinto, Jane Rawes and Tonny Shankland.

Thanks to Stephen Sheard of Rowan, Ken and June Bridgewater of Westminster Fibers, and their support staff for producing the glorious fabrics for the Kaffe Fassett Fabric Collection.

Huge thanks to the owners of our glorious photographic locations – Marilyn Phipps of The Battery; Rupert and Carolyn Spira of Church Farm, More; Princess Romanoff, Rye; Genetta Sindell, Withersham; Justin Cordwell, More; Parham House in West Sussex and the head gardener there; Mills Farm, Rye; Donald Evans for showing us Kirby Hall in Northamptonshire. Thanks also to the American Museum, Bath; the Bat Center, Durban, South Africa; Fonthill in Doylestown, Pennsylvania.

Special thanks for their support to Richard Womersley, Yvonne Mably, Margaret Hill, Susan Druding, Sandy Donabed, Victoria Slind-Flor, Judy Smith, Valerie Clarke, Deanna Apfel, Trubey Walker, the Roos and Lucy family.

Heartfelt thanks to the creative and patient book team – Polly Dawes, Debbie Patterson, Sally Harding, Denise Bates, Ethan Danielson and Jon Stewart.

For support, encouragement and most of all not minding living with thread, fabric and quilts EVERYWHERE, thanks to Liza's family, Drew, Alex and Elizabeth Lucy.

For neverending generosity of spirit and creative support, thanks to Brandon Mably.

photo credits

All of the photographs in this book were taken by Debbie Patterson, except for the patchwork flat shots (pages 72–142) which were taken by Jon Stewart.

supplier's credit

The footstool for the *Turban Footstool* on pages 67 and 136 was supplied by: Fleur De Paris, 8255 Beverly Boulevard, Los Angeles, CA 90048, USA.

ABOVE The subtle flower prints of the *Japanese Brocades* blending exquisitely with the old stone of Kirby Hall, an Elizabethan mansion near the village of Gretton in Northamptonshire, England.

kaffe fassett fabric collection

Kaffe Fassett has designed a range of pure cotton fabrics for patchwork. Some are prints, and others are woven on hand looms through the Fair Trading Trusts in India. No two hand woven fabrics are exactly identical, and the small imperfections in these cloths add to their handmade beauty.

Many of the quilts in the book contain some patches cut from KAFFE FASSETT fabrics and a few are made entirely from this fabric collection. You can, of course, make your own selection of fabrics for the patchworks, but if you would like to purchase any KAFFE FASSETT fabrics, see the addresses below.

UK
For details of stockists and mail order sources in the United Kingdom for the KAFFE FASSETT Fabric Collection, please contact the Rowan head office.

HEAD OFFICE: **Rowan**, Green Lane Mill, Holmfirth, West Yorkshire HD9 2DX, England. Tel: +44 (0) 1484 681 881. Fax: +44 (0) 1484 687 920. E-mail: Mail@knitrowan.com Website: **www.knitrowan.com**

EUROPE AND AUSTRALIA
Contact the distributors listed below for stockists of the KAFFE FASSETT Fabric Collection in Europe and Australia.

Australia
Sunspun, 185 Canterbury Road, Canterbury 3126, Victoria. Tel: 61 3 5979 1555. Fax: 61 3 5979 1544. E-mail: sunspun@labyrinth.net.au

Belgium, France, Germany and Holland
Rhinetex, Geurdeland 7, 6673 DR Andelst, Holland. Tel: 31 488 480030. Fax: 31 488 480422.

Denmark, Norway and Sweden
I C Waltersdorff & Co APS, Postboks 89, Charlottenlund Stationplads 7, DK 2920 Charlottenlund. Tel: 45 39 63 14 10. Fax: 45 39 64 44 58. E-mail: waltersdorff@adr.dk

Iceland
Malin Orglygsdottir, Garnverslunin Storkurinn, Kjorgardi Laugavegi 59, 101 Reykjavik. Tel: 354 551 82 58. Fax: 354 562 82 52.

Spain
Lucretia Beleta Patchwork, Dr Rizal 12, 08006 Barcelona. Tel: 34 93 415 9555. Fax: 34 93 415 5241. E-mail: lucrecia@1bpatchwork.com

Switzerland
Stoffe & Patchwork, Hauptstrasse 13, Ch 4436 Oberdorf. Tel: 41 61 961 1808. Fax: 41 963 0035. E-mail: hydrosolar@datacomm.ch

US
The KAFFE FASSETT Fabric Collection is available in many quilting stores across the United States. A few selected stores are listed below. For the location of a store nearer you, contact Westminster Fibers.

DISTRIBUTOR: **Westminster Fibers Inc**, 5 Northern Boulevard, Amherst, NH 03031. Tel: (603) 886-5041. Fax: (603) 886-1056. E-mail: wfibers@aol.com

California
• New Pieces, 1597 Solano Avenue, Berkeley, CA 94707. Tel: (510) 527-6779.

Minnesota
•The Sampler, 535 West 78th Street, Chanhassen, MN 55317. Tel: (612) 934-5307.

New Hampshire
• Portsmouth Fabric Company, 112 Penhallow Street, Portsmouth, NH 03801. Tel: (603) 436-6343.

Oregon
• Stitchin' Post, 311 W. Cascade Street, Sisters, OR 97759. Tel: (541) 549-6061

Washington
• Quiltworks Northwest, 145 106th Avenue, NE Bellevue, WA 98004-4610. Tel: (425) 453-6005. Website: **www.quiltworksnw.com**
• In The Beginning Fabrics, 8201 Lake City Way NE, Seattle, WA 98115. Tel: (206) 523-8862.

fabric stores

The following US stores sell many of the fabrics used in quilts in this book, including most of the KAFFE FASSETT Fabric Collection:

Maryland
• G Street Fabrics, 11854 Rockville Pike, Rockville, MD 20852. Tel: (301) 231-8998. Website: **www.gstreetfabrics.com**

New Jersey
• Quilt Connection, 432 F Springfield Avenue, Berkeley Heights, NJ 07922. Tel: (908) 286-0200. Website: **www.njquiltconnection.com**

Pennsylvania
• Country Quilt Shop, 515 Stump Road, Montgomeryville, PA 18936. Tel: (215) 855-5554 and (888) 627-6969. Website: **www.countryquiltshop.com**

Virginia
• G Street Fabrics, 5077 Westfields Boulevard, Centreville, VA 20120. Tel: (703) 818-8090.
• G Street Fabrics, 6250 Seven Corners Center, Falls Church, VA 22044. Tel: (703) 241-1700. Website: **www.gstreetfabrics.com**

EXOTIC FABRICS
For unusual African indigo cloth and other exotic fabrics:
• St. Theresa Textile Trove, Inc, 1329 Main Street, Cincinnati, OH 45210. Tel: (800) 236-2450 and (513) 333-0399. Fax: (513) 333-0012. For general information, e-mail: info@sttheresatextile.com

For South African indigo fabrics:
• Cotton In The Cabin, 17727 State Road 1, Spencerville, IN 46788. Tel: 219 238 4620. Website: **www.cottoninthecabin.com**

index